TURNAR

The Orthodox
Purpose Driven Life

A ONE MONTH LIFE STRATEGY
FOR SPIRITUAL RENEWAL

About The Author
Forrest Long was born in New Brunswick, Canada and served for twenty-eight years as a Baptist minister in churches in eastern Canada and the State of Maine. He presently lives in Alabama with his wife, Patsy. Forrest has two grown children and two grandsons. Along with his focus on ministry, Forrest has been on a personal spiritual journey, which ultimately brought him into contact with the Orthodox Church. Through counsel, prayer and study, he became Orthodox and was chrismated in the Antiochian Orthodox Church. He now attends St. Gregory the Theologian Orthodox Church in Tuscaloosa, Alabama. His time is devoted now to freelance writing and painting.

TURNAROUND

The Orthodox Purpose Driven Life

A ONE MONTH LIFE STRATEGY FOR SPIRITUAL RENEWAL

By

Forrest Long

Regina Orthodox Press
Salisbury, Massachusetts

Turnaround
ISBN 978-1-928653-30-1

© 2007 Forrest Long

Regina Orthodox Press
PO BOX 5288
Salisbury MA 01952

reginaorthodoxpress.com

This book is dedicated to my children, Angela and Matthew, in their personal spiritual journeys. May you fix your eyes on Jesus and model him in your lives.

TABLE of CONTENTS

WEEK FOUR- MINISTRY IN MOTION

TWO MORE DAYS: A NEW VISION

WEEK ONE
DAY ONE

WHO DO YOU KNOW?
A Preface: Charting The Course For Your Spiritual Journey

How is your spiritual health? Do you sometimes get the feeling that maybe you have neglected it, that like a garden it has become overrun with weeds and the soil lacks nourishment?

Do you have a sense at times that you are going through the motions and getting nowhere, or maybe even slipping back a bit? Have you ever found yourself saying- to yourself or to someone else- "If only I could get my hands on something that would bring real change to my spiritual life, something I could do myself!"

Jesus said, "I came that they may have life, and have it abundantly." (John 10:10). Have you read the verse before? Maybe you have known it for years. But right now your thought may be, "Somehow there is a vast difference between what Jesus says and the life I am living."

So often in the process of living we get bogged down in the details, the frustrations, and even the monotony of the daily grind, to the point that we can lose sight of the life Jesus Christ calls us to live. We devise ways of making it through. Some choose to wear a mask to hide the inner disappointment and emptiness. Some go through the motions but have long ago given up any expectation of experiencing such an abundant life, thinking that this is the best it will get. When we begin to think this way we begin to accept that this is average- everyone is this way.

Can you relate to this? Do you hunger for a genuine change in your life that will infuse your life with a greater sense of purpose and meaning as well as a greater sense of joy?

What price are you willing to pay to achieve that? Are you willing to begin by investing thirty-one days?

1

Just one month- in the overall scope of your life it's not a lot, but it could be the great beginning of a new you!

Now for a few disclaimers-

- You won't find anything here that hasn't been said before. There is no new teaching, no special revelation. Read the Scripture verses, the quotes, the assignments. These are all familiar, age-old truths that are put together to help you focus on where you want your life to be spiritually.
- It's only 31 days. The list isn't exhaustive. Probably other things could have been added. But one month is a beginning, "bite-size" chunks that are manageable. One month isn't forever, but it could very well impact your life forever.
- You have to do the work. There is no magic in this. You have to commit yourself to doing the daily work- blocking out necessary time and taking action one day at a time. Your effort will be rewarded.

The goal is CHANGE!

Each day focuses on a new biblical/spiritual concept in a practical way so that you can pick it up and run with it. My desire is not to overwhelm you with material but to give you a glimpse, get you thinking, get you focused, and hopefully ignite a fire that will burn inwardly and outwardly in your life. Change comes about by creating a new vision of what your life can be.

Each day represents a small trickle of a stream that runs into the next day, flowing together to build a mighty river in your life spiritually. You are never really done with a day at the end of your reading and application because these things must be incorporated into your life.

Keep a journal! This spiritual journey is designed to be recorded. Keep a daily journal. Record your answers to questions asked, but go beyond that- record your struggles, your fears, your questions and doubts, as well as what you are learning and how you are changing through the process. In the end you may just have a best seller for your life.

Before You Begin This Journey
A command, a promise and a prayer to get you started:
- *A command*: "Work out your own salvation with fear and trembling." (Philippians 2:12). Salvation is a life-long journey. With a sense of holy reverence for God ("fear and trembling") you are called to apply your salvation to all of your life.
- *A promise*: "For it is God who is at work in you, enabling you both to will and to work for His good pleasure" (Philippians 2:13). What great news! You're not on this journey alone! What you are about to begin, you begin with God. God desires to give you the will to continue and the strength to achieve. Remember this is a partnership- don't try to do it on your own!
- *A prayer*: Ephesians 1:15-23. Take time to read this prayer because it applies to you. It's a prayer for your well-being, that God, "May give you a spirit of wisdom and revelation as you come to know Him." There are three things you come to know through this spirit of wisdom and revelation: 1. "You may know the hope to which He has called you." 2. You may understand "what are the riches of His glorious inheritance among the saints." 3. You may come to discover "what is the immeasurable greatness of His power for us who believe."

Now here is something very basic and important to understand in relation to your faith journey in Christianity. You may be working through this book on your own, but you cannot live your faith on your own. It is essential that your Christian journey is experienced within the context of the Church. Our culture may be very much into individualism, but Christ calls us to be part of His Church. I would encourage you to seek out an

Orthodox Church in your city if you are not presently attending one. Learn the faith and grow in the faith within the context of the Church. You need the worship and fellowship, the sacraments, the discipline and direction that you can only receive from a local church.

Another aid on your spiritual journey is the wisdom and direction of a spiritual mentor, one who is mature in the faith and able to give you wise direction, help you with your questions and struggles, establish a discipline for you on your journey. This person may be your priest, a mature believer within the congregation who has the time to invest in your life, or someone locally the church can recommend for you. This person will be invaluable to your journey. Develop a relationship in which you can bare your heart and soul to this person, trust their wisdom and judgment, as well as have confidence in their leadership. God bless you as you embark on this life-changing journey.

WEEK ONE
DAY TWO

GOD INESCAPABLE

Scripture For The Day
        Psalm 139:7-12
        Where can I go from your Spirit? Or where can I flee from
Your presence? If I ascend to heaven, You are there; if I make my
bed in hell, behold You are there. If I take the wings of the
morning, and dwell in the uttermost parts of the sea, even there
Your hand shall lead me, and Your right hand shall hold me. If I
say, "Surely the darkness shall fall on me," even the night shall be
light about me; indeed the darkness shall not hide You, but the
night shines as the day; the darkness and the light are both alike to
You.

Quote For The Day
St. Symeon, The New Theologian
        I know that the Immovable comes down;
        I know that the Invisible appears to me;
        I know that he who is far outside the whole creation
        Takes me within himself and hides me in his arms,
        And then I find myself outside the whole world.
        I, a frail, small mortal in the world,
        Behold the Creator of the world, all of Him, within myself;
        And I know that I shall not die, for I am within the Life,
        I have the whole of Life springing up as a fountain within me.
        He is in my heart, He is in heaven:
        Both there and here He shows Himself to me with equal glory. [2]

Reflect On This

Do you ever want to be just alone? You know the feeling-to escape the intrusion of words, sounds and activity, to spend some solitary time. We all long for that at times, retreating into silence with a longing to experience peacefulness, to put our mind at ease and our soul at rest. How spiritually and emotionally invigorating a mini retreat can be, even if it may last for only a few minutes in the midst of a hectic day.

Can we ever be truly alone? The psalmist in our verses for the day presents an image of one trying their best to escape God's presence, for whatever reason. Maybe he was seeking to hide from God like Adam and Eve after their disobedience in the garden. But the psalmist paints a much larger picture, not simply trying to hide from God behind a tree. He discovers that God's presence is inescapable wherever he could go, from the heights of heaven to the depths of the place of the dead, to the farthest limits of the sea, even into the blackest darkness. Why would he want to escape? Could it be like Adam and Eve a matter of guilt. It's interesting how we react to guilt, not only in relation to people but before God as well. Guilt makes us uncomfortable in the presence of a holy God, yet that presence is inescapable.

Sometimes we fear being alone. How often children fear being alone at night in the dark. Can you remember back to fears like this? What comfort there would be in having a night light or the bedroom door left open at night. God's inescapable presence can be a source of comfort and blessing, even as expressed so beautifully by St. Symeon in his hymn quoted for today. To realize our smallness and seeming insignificance in the vast expanse of all that exists can create a sense of loneliness and fear. As immense and incomprehensible as God is, yet this great God is a personal God who knows each of us. Jesus responds to our human fears with these words that give us a glimpse into the inescapable presence of a loving and caring God, "Are not two sparrows sold for a penny? Yet not one of them will fall to the ground apart from

6

your Father. And even the hairs of your head are all counted. So do not be afraid; you are of more value than many sparrows." (Matthew 10:29-31).

It's an impossibility to know everything about God, for to do so we would have to be God. Our capacity for knowing is limited because we are finite and God is infinite. Out of that reality we sometimes make the mistake of imagining God to be much like us. Foolishly we may reason, if I can hide something from other people, I can hide it from God, and we fail to understand that before God "the darkness shall not hide from You." (Psalm 139:12). On the other hand you may find yourself in a situation where you feel no one cares about you and it can be easy to move from there to think that God doesn't care either. But God does care! This God is a personal God Who has been where we are in Jesus Christ, to understand our pain, feel our loneliness. The words of St. Symeon express that reality in such a beautiful and profound way. This is our God!

Think, Respond And Apply

1. Do you ever find yourself running from God, looking for a place to hide? Try to recall a particular incident. What caused you to react that way and what was the outcome?

2. Do you struggle with loneliness and fear? In your personal relationships what brings on these feelings? What would you like to tell God when you feel overwhelmed by loneliness or fear? What do you look for from God?

3. Stop and reflect in silence. Are there things in your life that you are hiding from God, maybe something from yesterday, or something that has been hiding in a dark corner of your soul for years? Talk to God about it. Go to your priest in confession. Be willing to let go of it in confession and forgiveness.

4. Your assignment- This week intentionally plan to take a mini-retreat. Get alone, even if it's just for an hour. Read and reflect on Psalm 139. Write down what you learn about God from

this psalm. How does this make you feel about yourself? From what you discover in the psalm, what does it make you want to change in your relationship with God? Be specific and write this down to remember. Bring the time to a close by making the request of verses 23 and 24 your prayer.

Pray
The old saying "confession is good for the soul" is much more than just an old saying. In the light of what you have considered today, come to God with your fears and your guilt, things you know right now that you are struggling with. Confess them to God. Seek the peace Christ promised you. Then move on, leave those things with God and don't carry them any further yourself.

WEEK ONE
DAY THREE

IS THIS MY GOD?

Scripture For The Day
Isaiah 40:25-28
To whom then will you liken Me, or to whom shall I be equal?
says the Holy One. Lift up your eyes on high, and see who has
created these things, who brings out their host by number; He calls
them all by name; by the greatness of His might and the strength of
His power; not one is missing. Why do you say, O Jacob, and
speak, O Israel: "My way is hidden from the Lord, and my just
claim is passed over by my God?" Have you not known? Have you
not heard? The everlasting God, the Lord, the Creator of the ends
of the earth, neither faints nor is weary. His understanding is
unsearchable.

Quote For The Day
St. John Cassian
        When we reflect on the measurelessness of His power and
His unsleeping eye which looks upon the hidden things of the heart
and which nothing can escape, we are filled with the deepest awe,
marveling at Him and adoring Him. When we consider that He
numbers the raindrops, the sand of the sea and the stars of heaven,
we are amazed at the grandeur of His nature and His wisdom.
When we think of His ineffable and inexplicable wisdom, His love
for mankind, and his limitless long-suffering at man's innumerable
sins, we glorify Him. When we consider His great love for us, in
that though we had done nothing good, He, being God, deigned to
become man in order to save us from delusion, we are roused to
longing for Him. When we reflect that He Himself has vanquished
in us our adversary, the devil, and that He has given us eternal life

if only we would choose and turn toward His goodness, then we venerate Him. [3]

Reflect On This

What is there in the natural world that takes your breath away? Is it the majesty of the mountains, the raging surf at the ocean's edge, the beauty of a sunset, or the vastness of the universe viewed in a clear night's sky? In spite of all the destruction, ugliness and suffering in our world, there is still such a sense of beauty and grandeur that it causes us to stand in silent awe. It's that view that for the first time or the hundredth time takes our breath away. What is it for you? Close your eyes as you think about it and picture it in your mind.

The vastness and complexities of creation boggles our minds at times. In many ways it's beyond even the scope of our imagination- for example as we contemplate the vastness of space. The figures of distance alone are staggering. Yet the Bible tells us that God has created all of this and sustains it continually. Our God is greater than all of creation around us. So many things in creation are beyond our minds to comprehend, yet the wisdom and mind of God has conceived of and created all that exists. Sometimes in our contemplation of God we lose sight of this fact.

Think of that natural scene that takes your breath away and causes you to stand before it in awe. Now think of God. Have you ever had that same sense of awe as you ponder the God you believe in, worship and serve? Unfortunately sometimes our concept of God the Creator is smaller than our understanding of all that is apart from God, all of creation.

"Lift up your eyes on high and see: who created these? He who brings out their host and numbers them, calling them all by name; because he is great in strength, mighty in power, not one is missing." Isaiah 40:26

Ponder that statement of Scripture for a moment and let its implications sink into your mind. Space is so vast that there are stars we have yet to see and planets still to be discovered, galaxies beyond the reach of our most powerful telescopes. Yet God knows them all, has put them in place and sustains them- "not one is missing." Space is mind-boggling, breathtaking. It all exists and is there because of God. Are you missing the connection? Think about the words of today's quote as St John Cassian portrays our great God- "the measurelessness of His power and His unsleeping eye... the grandeur of His nature and His wisdom...His limitless long-suffering... His great love for us..." Is this how you see God? If not maybe your God is too small. You need to see the God of Isaiah in all of His majesty, glory and power. This is our God!

Think, Respond And Apply

1. Most people have never had an Isaiah 6 encounter with God. Take some time to think about you personal encounters with God. Is there an occasion that stands out in your mind as "breathtaking," a time when you sensed how awesome God is?

2. Think of some adjectives that you would use to describe your daily relationship with God and write them down. How do you feel about the adjectives you chose and what picture do they paint of your relationship with God?

3. What part does worship play in your life? Is it a Sunday only activity or does it have a place each day? Think of ways you could make worship a more focal part of your daily life, especially in relation to your devotional and prayer life.

4. Your assignment- Over the next week make a point to reflect on God when you notice the beauty of creation around you. It may be a beautiful sunrise or sunset, the beauty of the flowers, the cheerful song of a bird, the starry sky at night, beauty you see in the face of someone you love, or any number of things. The list can be endless. If you have opportunity, write down your reflections on God in these things.

Pray

In 1 Kings 6:15-17, the prophet Elisha and his servant were in the town of Dothan and found themselves under attack by the Syrian army. The servant was fearful of what was about to happen, but Elisha prayed, "Lord, I pray, open his eyes that he might see." God answered Elisha's prayer and the servant's eyes were open to see the army of heaven there to protect them.

Maybe you need to begin praying, "Lord, open my eyes that I may see You." Pray that God would open the eyes of your soul to behold the majesty and glory of God. Pray too that God may open your heart to respond daily in adoration and praise. In your daily praying begin putting adoration and praise ahead of your "to do" list for God and see what a difference it makes.

WEEK ONE
DAY FOUR

DOES GOD HAVE COMPETITION?

Scripture For The Day
Psalm 63:1-5
O God, You are my God, early will I seek You; my soul thirsts for
You; my flesh longs for you, in a dry and thirsty land where there
is no water. So I have looked for You in the sanctuary, to see Your
power and glory. Because Your lovingkindness is better than life,
my lips shall praise You. Thus I will bless you while I live; I will
lift up my hands to Your name. My soul shall be satisfied as with
marrow and fatness, and my mouth shall praise You with joyful
lips.

Quote For The Day
Augustine of Hippo (Confessions)
        You made us for Yourself and our hearts find no peace
until they rest in You. Who will grant me to rest content in You?
To whom shall I turn for the gift of Your coming into my heart and
filling it to the brim, so that I may not forget all the wrong I have
done and embrace You alone, my only source of good?
        Why do You mean so much to me? Help me to find words
to explain. Why do I mean so much to You, that You should
command me to love you?... Tell me why You mean so much to
me. Whisper in my heart, I am here to save You. Speak so I may
hear Your words...
        My soul is like a house, small for You to enter, but I pray
You to enlarge it. It is in ruins, but I ask You to remake it. It
contains much that You will not be pleased to see: this I know and
do not hide. But who is to rid it of these things? There is no one
but You to whom I can say: if I have sinned unwittingly, do You
absolve me? [4]

13

Reflect On This

We live in a very competitive world. The continual assault of marketing and advertising from all directions gives us a daily reminder of this reality. And it works. We are all consumers and the marketing strategy influences our daily decisions from the breakfast cereal we eat to the toothpaste we use, the designer clothes we wear, the car we drive, the bank we use, and the list goes on. Even churches have plugged into the competitive marketplace and often function with their own marketing strategy. Competition and the urge to find a better product. It's an endless cycle today.

Does God face competition in your life, along with everything else? The quote for the day contains one of the most famous lines from Augustine- "You made us for Yourself and our hearts find no peace until they rest in You." Someone has described the human heart as having a God-shaped space that nothing else or no one else other than God can fill. And until that space is properly filled there will be a discontent of soul. Yet strangely enough today, too many people who profess to be Christians exhibit a real sense of discontent and seem to be on a continual search for something more. It may be a search for a deeper experience, more meaningful worship, a more lively church, but it is an ongoing search for something more to meet their needs. Maybe the question needs to be asked, "Have you never discovered what it is to have your soul fully satisfied in God alone?" Is this an issue you are presently struggling with? Is there a sense of emptiness or dissatisfaction in your soul which causes you to look beyond God to fill?

The psalmist David expressed his great hunger for God in our Scripture today- "O God, You are my God, early will I seek You, my soul thirsts for You; my flesh longs for You in a dry and thirsty land where there is no water." (Psalm 63:1). We all get

14

thirsty at times, but do you know the thirst of someone dying in a desert? That's the image we have here. That's thirst, but the physical image conveys a spiritual reality: we are to have that degree of thirst of soul for God. This is a thirst that only God can quench and once God quenches that thirst there is no need to look any further. The result is expressed so beautifully in another word picture- "My soul shall be satisfied as with marrow and fatness, and my mouth shall praise You with joyful lips." (63:5).

"My soul shall be satisfied." How many people today could honestly make that statement? There are probably many even within the church who would find it difficult to say without some reservation. Could it be that for someone who is a Christian, God isn't enough to satisfy their soul? But maybe the problem doesn't rest with God. The message of Scripture is that God is sufficient for our needs, even the deepest needs of our soul and our salvation. The psalmist writes, "Because Your lovingkindness is better than life, my lips shall praise You." (63:3). God's love is steadfast; it never weakens or wavers; it's not here today and gone tomorrow. God's love is poured out to us in mercy, forgiveness, acceptance and soul-satisfying fullness.

What are you looking for? Maybe you have not come to fully understand all that you have in having God. Maybe in your ongoing search your soul has become cluttered with lesser things that narrow the space God occupies in your life.

Think, Respond And Apply
1. Augustine said in the quote, "My soul is like a house." Reflect on that image for a few minutes in relation to your soul. If God dwells in the "house" of your soul, does He feel comfortable or crowded there? Is there need to do some soul work in order to give God more space? Where can you begin?

2. Do you recognize a sense of hungering for God in your heart? Does that feeling arise in worship, during your devotional times or at other times in your life? Do you find yourself crying

15

out to God like the psalmist, "O God, You are my God, I seek You, my soul thirsts for You"?

3. Do you wrestle with dissatisfaction and frustration in your spiritual life? What would you like God to do to help you? Can you see a solution that may involve a cooperative effort between you and God?

4. What is there about God that fills your heart with joy and praise? Take time to reflect on this and write down the things that come to mind. These are important things to always remember.

Pray

In reflecting on your level of spiritual satisfaction in God, open your heart in praise and thanksgiving. At the same time be honest about your struggles. If there are things in your life that you have allowed to compete with God, come to terms with them and confess it to God. Pray that the Holy Spirit who dwells within you will search your soul and let you know where housecleaning needs to be done. Pray that your hunger for God will increase.

WEEK ONE
DAY FIVE

GOD IS LOVE

Scriptures For The Day
Romans 5:6-8
For when we were still without strength, in due time Christ died for the ungodly. For scarcely for a righteous man will one die; yet perhaps for a good man someone would even dare to die. But God demonstrates His own love toward us, in that while we were still sinners Christ died for us.
1 John 4:9,10
In this the love of God was manifested toward us, that God sent His only begotten Son into the world, that we might live through Him. In this is love, not that we loved God, but that He loved us and sent His Son to be the propitiation for our sins.

Quote For The Day
Fr. Theoklitos of Dionysiou
        Believe me, there is one truth that reigns supreme from the fringes of the throne of glory down to the least shadow of the most insignificant of creatures: and that one truth is love. Love is the source from which the holy streams of grace flow down unceasingly from the city of God, watering the earth and making it fruitful.... It is love that fashions all things and holds them in unity. It is love that gives life and warmth, that inspires and guides. Love is the seal set upon creation, the signature of the Creator. Love is the explanation of His handiwork. 5

Reflect On This
        Does God have any idea what I'm going through? Does God actually care about me and understand my needs? Do these questions ever run through your mind? Do you sometimes wrestle

with your own sense of smallness and insignificance in the scope of all humanity and the vastness of all existence beyond our tiny planet? It may seem inconceivable to you that a God who is great enough to create all of this would take any thought of you and your need.

The majesty and greatness of God are topics of Scripture, from the creation account of Genesis, to the praise and worship of the psalms, to the great events of the end of the age in Revelation. Between the two bookends of creation and re-creation, the pages of Scripture reveal to us a personal God Who is gracious and merciful, loving and caring. God is confronted by a humanity in rebellion and sin, yet we see that this God is neither helpless nor frustrated. The amazing fact is that God acts in such a way to reveal the depth of divine love and mercy that is truly amazing.

One of the most familiar verses of the whole Bible is John 3:16, "For God so loved the world that he gave his only Son…" Romans 5:6-8 follows in the spirit of that verse and expands on the great proclamation of love. Verse eight tells us, "But God proves his love for us in that while we were still sinners Christ died for us." Think of that- "God proves his love." The old saying is, "talk is cheap". God has spoken and Jesus Christ is God's ultimate word to us. It was far more than just words. The love of God was loudly proclaimed through a manger, in the villages and hillsides of Israel and ultimately from a cross. That was love in action costly, committed, sacrificial love.

John tells us that God in essence is love, expressed concisely in three words- "God is love." (1 John 4:8) He then explains how that love was revealed to us: "God's love was revealed among us in this way: God sent His only Son into the world so that we might live through him." (4:9) The ultimate expression of that love was the cross, for God "Sent His Son to be the atoning sacrifice for our sins." (4:10)

Does God understand pain and suffering? In a most profound way, beyond our ability to ever comprehend, God understands pain and suffering, rejection and ridicule. God understands because He has been here where we are. The compassion of God is seen in Jesus Christ as He reached out to the poor, the outcasts, the suffering and the sinners; loving them, accepting them, and transforming their lives with hope. The heart of God is seen in Jesus as He wept over the city of Jerusalem, as He approached the grave of His dear friend Lazarus, as He prayed in agony in the garden on that final night.

"God is love" is not simply a pious platitude to be put on a plaque and hung on the wall. At the greatest possible personal price God loves, and that love reaches out to you, offering you forgiveness, hope and peace.

Think, Respond And Apply

1. Are there times in your life when you are caused to wonder if God really understands your need and cares? How do you feel at those times and how do you deal with those feelings?

2. Do you ever have difficulty understanding that God's love is personal, that God loves you as an individual? Do personal feelings of unworthiness or insignificance help create this difficulty?

3. The quote for today says, "Love is the source from which the holy streams of grace flow down unceasingly from the city of God, watering the earth and making it fruitful." Stop and reflect on the magnitude of love expressed by God in so many ways, including sending Christ to the cross for you. What thoughts are going through your mind as you ponder this?

4. Take some time to think seriously about your personal experiences of pain, loneliness, or loss, things that may have caused you to wonder if God understands and cares. When you are finished reflect on what you have written in the light of what you considered today about God's costly love for you. When you look at your trials in the light of the cross and the love of God can you see things from a different perspective?

Pray

　　"Love" can be such a superficial and overworked word that becomes emptied of its meaning. Yet there are situations and actions in which love is revealed in a most profound way. Quiet your heart in the presence of God and reflect on the costly, sacrificial love that God has expressed to you. Pray that God would open your eyes to see in a clearer way the immensity of love poured out from the heart of God through Jesus. Bring to God your doubts and frustrations, even your anger you may have felt at times. Ask God for healing and to replace those feelings and fears with the peace of Christ and being settled in His love for you.

WEEK ONE
DAY SIX

THE SURPASSING VALUE OF KNOWING CHRIST

Scripture For The Day
Philippians 3:7-11
But what things were gain to me, I counted loss for Christ. Yet
indeed I also count all things loss for the excellence of the
knowledge of Christ Jesus my Lord, for whom I have suffered the
loss of all things, and count them as rubbish, that I may gain Christ
and be found in Him, not having my own righteousness, which is
from the law, but that which is through faith in Christ, the
righteousness which is from God by faith; that I may know Him
and the power of His resurrection, and the fellowship of His
sufferings, being conformed to His death, if, by any means, I may
attain to the resurrection from the dead.

Quote For The Day
Symeon, the New Theologian
　　My Christ,
　　You are the Kingdom of Heaven,
　　You are the land promised to the meek,
　　You are the meadows of paradise,
　　The hall of celestial banquet,
　　The ineffable bridal chamber,
　　The table open for all comers.
　　You are the bread of life,
　　The wonderful new drink,
　　The cool jar of water,
　　The water of life.
　　You are the lamp
　　That never goes out for all your saints,
　　The new garment, the diadem,

21

The one who distributes diadems.
You are our joy and repose,
our delight and glory.
You are gladness and laughter, my God.
Your grace, the grace of the all-holy Spirit,
shines in the saints like a blazing sun. [6]

Reflect On This

Remember "doubting Thomas"? Who could forget him; his name has been memorialized by that one act of doubt recorded in the gospel. "Unless I see for myself; unless I can reach out and touch, I will not believe." But what an encounter he finally had with the risen Christ. "Thomas, reach out and touch my hand- the nail scars. Put your hand here where the spear pierced my side. Thomas, I'm alive; it's me, Jesus." All Thomas could do was bow in humble adoration with the words, "My Lord and my God!" (John 20:28). From that amazing encounter when all doubts were wiped away, Thomas went on with the other apostles to proclaim the gospel of the living Christ.

Then there was the Apostle Paul, "Formerly a blasphemer, a persecutor, and an insolent man," (1 Timothy 1:13) transformed by an encounter with the living Christ on the Damascus Road. What a different man we see in the historic record of the Book of Acts as well as in his epistles. As we see in our Scripture for today, to the converted Saul of Tarsus Jesus Christ had become the greatest treasure of his life. He never came to Christ out of a life of failure and defeat. His life had been one of accomplishment and esteem in the eyes of his peers. His authority and power caused dread in the hearts of Christians whom he persecuted. After his encounter with Christ he looks back on all his accomplishments and says, "But what things were gain to me, these I have counted loss for Christ…. for Whom I have suffered the loss of all things, and count them as rubbish, that I may gain Christ." (Philippians 3:7,8)

22

Gain and loss, surpassing value and rubbish. Here was a person who discovered in Christ the richest treasure he could possibly have. There was nothing to compare with having Jesus Christ as Savior and in the end not even his life would be of that great a value. He speaks of "the excellence of the knowledge of Christ Jesus my Lord" a knowledge that was above and beyond anything else he had known or could know. That knowledge implied a saving, life-changing relationship.

What do you treasure in your life, by way of persons or possessions? If you are a Christian can you honestly say that you treasure Christ above all else? Can you relate to Paul's great desire, "That I may gain Christ and be found in him...I want to know Christ and the power of his resurrection and the sharing of his sufferings..." Is Jesus Christ the treasure of your life?

Read again the quote for today, the words of St. Symeon the New Theologian as he was known. Symeon, who lived in Constantinople from 949 to 1022, turned from an aristocratic lifestyle to follow Christ and become a monk and a great mystic-poet. His words today reflect how very much he treasured Jesus Christ. "My Christ, You are..." It was personal, life-transforming, all-consuming, knowing this living Christ personally.

Many who profess to follow Christ prefer to follow at a distance or compartmentalize their life so that Christ is supposedly contained in one little room. Until you come to see Jesus Christ as the greatest treasure of your life and hold in highest esteem the surpassing value of knowing Christ, you will never truly know what it is to follow Him.

Think, Respond And Apply

1. Do you ever have the sense of being overwhelmed in your heart by the Greatness of Christ's love to you and the extent to which He went to prove that love? Out of those thoughts how do you respond to Christ, not just in words but with your life?

2. In your life what do you count as "loss" because of Christ? Do you see it as a great price to pay to follow Christ as His disciple? Do you sometimes find yourself struggling with issues of ownership in your life?

3. There is a difference in how you treasure an object and how you treasure a person. Think of someone in your life whom you truly treasure, someone very dear to you. Because of the place that person holds in your heart how do you treat them? Now focus your attention on Jesus Christ, your Savior and Lord. How have you been treating Him in your life? If He is truly the treasure of your heart how should you express it? What changes do you have to make?

4. Read again the quote for today. These are such beautiful words coming from the heart of one who truly treasured Christ. Now take a piece of paper or your journal and write "My Christ" at the top. Fill in the rest with what comes from your heart as you reflect.

Pray

So often we forget to make adoration a regular part of our prayers. They may get off-balanced with our needs and desires we bring to God. Right now come to Jesus Christ with your praise and worship. Express to him your love and adoration, your desire to glorify him with your life. Make this time of prayer a time of worship.

WEEK ONE
DAY SEVEN

THE SPIRIT, MY GUIDE

Scripture For The Day
John 16:12-15
I still have many things to say to you but you cannot bear them
now. However when He, the Spirit of truth has come, He will
guide you into all truth; for He will not speak on His own
authority, but whatever He hears He will speak, and He will tell
you the things to come. He will glorify me, for He will take of
what is Mine and declare it to you. All things that the Father has
are Mine. Therefore I said that He will take of mine and declare it
to you.

Quote For The Day
Niketas Stethatos (a monk at the famous Studium monastery
at Constantinople in the 12th century. He was a leader in the east in
the great controversy that led to the Great Schism between the east
and the west in 1054.)

> The Spirit is light, life and peace. If you are illuminated by
> the divine Spirit, your life will be established in peaceful
> serenity. A spring will gush out within you, which is the
> wisdom of the Logos and the mystical knowledge of
> existent being, and you will come to have the mind of
> Christ. Then you will know the mysteries of the Kingdom
> of God and will enter the depths of the deity, day by day
> speaking words of life for others from a heart that is calmed
> and enlightened.

Reflect On This

Have you ever tried to find your way around a room in the dark? If you are familiar with the room in the daylight it may not be too difficult, but if you are somewhere that is unfamiliar it could be a challenge. Obstacles in the way could bring your progress to a standstill. Life can be much like that.

When Jesus was confronted by a man who had been blind from birth, never able to find his own way around or see what was ahead of him, he said, "As long as I am in the world, I am the light of the world." (John 9:5). But the day came when Jesus physically left this world, yet as he had promised in the words of our Scripture today, he sent the Holy Spirit to be light for us, to direct us in the way of Christ.

Christians are not self-made people. The Bible is not a self-help manual to direct us in a do-it-yourself Christian life. What we are called to be in Christ is a human impossibility to construct on our own. We are told in 2 Corinthians 5:17, "Therefore if anyone is in Christ, he is a new creation: old things have passed away: behold, all things have become new." That is the miracle of being a Christian, being a new creation in Christ.

Conversion is the beginning, the entry into salvation, but as the Apostle Peter tells us, God continues to provide for us from that point onward, "His divine power has given to us all things that pertain to life and godliness, through the knowledge of Him who called us by glory and virtue." (2 Peter 1:3).

That's amazing! By God's power you now have all you need for life and godliness, all you need to become the person God desires you to be. Yet this isn't a self-help project that you can accomplish on your own. It is evident in the New Testament that we need one another as members of Christ's body, the Church, to grow together, but even that isn't enough. The message of Jesus, reinforced by the message of the New Testament epistles, is that we need the Holy Spirit working in us to become all that God desires us to be. It is a work of inner transformation that produces

26

outward change. That transformation process is compared to the ongoing changes we see by looking in a mirror- "But we all, with unveiled face, beholding as in a mirror the glory of the Lord, are being transformed into the same image from glory to glory; just as by the Spirit of the Lord." (2 Corinthians 3:18).

Jesus tells us in our Scripture today that the Holy Spirit came to inform us of all this, as well as bring about the necessary change. What Jesus began the Holy Spirit continues. Jesus laid the foundation, the means of change through His death and resurrection. The Holy Spirit makes the application of that change a reality in our lives. Jesus said of the Spirit, "He will guide you into all the truth... He will glorify me... He will take what is mine and declare it to you."

In the quote for today we are told "The Spirit is light, life and peace." The Holy Spirit came to guide us in the way God wants us to go, to give us the wisdom we need on the journey, and to bring about the ongoing transformation of life that is needed to live a life that radiates the glory of Christ to others. It's the work of the Holy Spirit that enables us to be the light of the world (Matthew 5:14-16).

May your goal not be to be a self-made person, but ultimately to be a God-made person, by the power of the Holy Spirit, for the glory of Jesus Christ.

Think, Respond And Apply

1. Do you get discouraged by your lack of spiritual growth and development? How have you progressed over the past year? What obstacles do you face in your spiritual growth?

2. How do you see your Christian life as a self-help project or as a cooperative effort with the Holy Spirit? How conscious are you of your need to depend on the Holy Spirit for direction as well as power to become all God wants you to be?

3. The Holy Spirit doesn't bring about your spiritual development and growth in isolation. We grow together as

members of the body of Christ, the Church, as we are told in Ephesians 4:11-16. What active part does the Church play in your spiritual growth? And in turn, how are you adding to the growth of the church (not simply in terms of numbers)?

4. Take time to read and meditate on the quote for today. Do you see in these words a goal for your own spiritual life and the person you desire to become? Write down some of your personal aspirations that may come to pass as the Holy Spirit works in your life.

Pray

The Holy Spirit as the Third Person of the Triune God can receive our prayers and our praise. Focus your thoughts and your prayer today on the Holy Spirit. Express your thankfulness for what is happening in your life. As well, express your desire for what you would like to become, for change that still needs to take place. Acknowledge your dependence on the Holy Spirit for this to happen. Make a verbal commitment to work together with the Spirit to make this a reality in your life.

WEEK TWO
DAY EIGHT

I MATTER TO GOD

Scripture For The Day
Psalm 8
O Lord, our Lord, how excellent is Your name in all the earth,
Who have set Your glory above the heavens! Out of the mouth of
babes and nursing infants You have ordained strength, because of
Your enemies, that You may silence the enemy and the avenger.
When I consider Your heavens, the work of Your fingers, the
moon and the stars, which You have ordained, what is man that
You are mindful of him, and the son of man that You visit him?
You have made him a little lower than the angels, and You have
crowned him with glory and honor. You have made him to have
dominion over the works of Your hands; you have put all things
under his feet, all sheep and oxen- even the beasts of the field, the
birds of the air, and the fish of the sea that pass through the paths
of the seas. O Lord, our Lord, how excellent is Your name in all
the earth!

Quote For The Day
Kallistos Ware (The Orthodox Way)
 Human beings are not counters that can be exchanged for
one another, or replaceable parts of a machine. Each, being free, is
unrepeatable; and each, being unrepeatable, is infinitely precious.
Human persons are not to be measured quantitatively; we have no
right to assume that one particular person is of more value than any
other particular person, or that ten persons must necessarily be of
more value than one. Such calculations are an offense to authentic
personhood. Each is irreplaceable, and therefore each must be
treated as an end in his or her self, and never as a means to some
further end. Each is to be regarded not as object but as subject. [8]

Reflect On This

In our postmodern and supposedly progressive secular culture people still cry out for meaning, significance and reason for being. The response is often a very loud silence. Through the marvels of modern communications and media we are inundated with video clips that scream "insignificance"- the rising body count of nameless faceless statistics in the unending succession of wars, uprisings and aggression, of crime in the streets and domestic violence. The media coverage is so efficient that too often we have become desensitized to the horror of such reality. These statistics are unique, irreplaceable human beings.

Do you ever find yourself saying, "Enough!" and turn off the remote? Does such a flow of depressing news ever cause you to wonder about the value and significance of human life, even your own? How do you view your own personal significance? You may have a "significant other" to whom you are of great value; children and other family members who value you; wider circles of friends, work associates and others who may be involved in your life on a regular basis and see you as a valued person. But what about your ultimate, eternal significance?

"When I consider Your heavens, the work of Your fingers, the moon and the stars which You have ordained; what is man that You are mindful of him, and the son of man that you visit him?" (Psalm 8:3,4). So it's an age-old question: What is the value of my life? The psalmist in our Scripture gives a very positive response to the question, a response you need to understand as you seek to comprehend your personal value in the grand view of things.

God created you, just a little lower than heavenly beings, crowned you with glory and honor, gave you a place of dominion over creation. God created us to show forth the splendor of divine glory and respond in worship and adoration. You are created in the image of God as a person of intelligence, creativity, freedom of will, and a soul that can enjoy communion with God. As the quote

30

for today says of each of us, "Each, being free, is unrepeatable; and each, being unrepeatable, is infinitely precious." Not only are you precious to those who know and love you here, you are also infinitely precious to God. The cross is ample proof of that.

You matter to God! Nor only is your life infinitely precious to God, but if you were to read through the Psalms you would discover how very much God cares for you, watches over you, and desires the very best for you. It's so easy to get down on yourself, to wonder if you or anything you do really matters. Believe that it does! God has said that it does, in imprinting your life with the divine image, in providing for you each day of life, in sending Jesus Christ to be your Savior and go to the cross to redeem you. If you didn't matter to God why would God even bother at all?

There is no greater issue to settle in coming to understand yourself than to be able to look in the mirror and say, "Yes! My life has value, purpose and meaning! I matter to God and others! What I do with my life is important!" Now, live your life in the light of that great reality.

Think, Respond And Apply

1. Have you ever had a time in your life, maybe as a child or even as an adult, when someone has put you down by telling you that you were stupid or couldn't do anything right? How did this make you feel at the time? Has it had any lasting impact on your life? Are there times when you may do something wrong and the words come back to haunt you?

2. How important is it to you to please those who have a significant place in your life? Do you look for their affirmation and approval? How do you feel when you let them down?

3. Focus on one statement from today's quote, "Each [person] being free, is unrepeatable; and each, being unrepeatable, is infinitely precious." When you stop and realize that statement is about you, how does it make you feel? What does it do for your self-image?

31

4. To know that your life matters to God and is of infinite value and importance; how does this affect what you do? Consider it in relation to your personal relationships, your spiritual life, your job, your leisure time.

Pray

If you struggle with issues of self-esteem and value in your life, bring these matters before God in prayer. Be honest and open about your struggles, knowing that God does care and can enable you to overcome them. Lay down those struggles before God and ask that you may have eyes to see yourself as God sees you, with the true value and potential that is there.

WEEK TWO
DAY NINE

UNCOVERING MY HEART

Scriptures For The Day
Jeremiah 17:9
The heart is deceitful above all things, and desperately wicked;
who can know it?
1 Samuel 16:7
But the Lord said to Samuel, "Do not look at his appearance or at
his physical stature, because I have refused him; for the Lord does
not see as man sees; for man looks at the outward appearance, but
the Lord looks at the heart."
Proverbs 3:5,6
Trust in the Lord with all your heart, and lean not on your own
understanding. In all your ways acknowledge Him and He shall
direct your paths.
Proverbs 21:2
Every way of man is right in his own eyes, but the Lord weighs the
hearts.
Proverbs 23:17
Do not let your heart envy sinners, but be zealous for the fear of
the Lord all the day.
Proverbs 27:19
As in water face reflects face, so a man's heart reveals the man.

Quote For The Day
        Makarios the Great (an anonymous Syrian master of the
spiritual life from the late 4th and early 5th centuries)
The heart itself is only a small vessel, yet dragons are there, and
lions, there are poisonous beasts and all the treasures of evil;
there are rough and uneven roads; there are precipices;

but there, too, are God and the angels; life is there, and the Kingdom; there, too, is light, and there are the apostles, and heavenly cities, and treasures of grace. All things lie within that little space.

Reflect On This

The book of Proverbs contains much wisdom concerning the human heart. Although you find no definition there of what the heart is, you soon discover by what is written that the human heart is the seat of our emotions, desires, will and affections. You could say it is the heart of your being, who you really are from the inside out.

Sometimes we are quick to judge people by outward appearances and later have to admit we were wrong. We discover in our Scripture for today, in 1 Samuel 16:7 the Lord responds to the prophet Samuel, who is seeking among the sons of Jesse for a king to replace King Saul as ruler of Israel. Samuel could see good prospects, but the Lord warned him not to be taken in by outward appearance but to look inwardly, for the Lord looks on the heart. The final choice was surprising, yet it was God's choice- David. Now we discover in the record of David's life that he wasn't a perfect man, yet he had a heart for the Lord.

The word "heart" is an interesting term. In our modern culture it has been so romanticized that our understanding of it can be very limited in scope, especially in comparison to the use of the word in the Bible. We discover, even in the few verses we have for our Scripture today, that the heart can be a source of good and evil.

Makarios, in the quote for today, uses great images and word pictures to help us have a larger understanding of the human heart. Some reflect "the treasures of evil" such as Jesus warned us of in Matthew 15:19. These are the dragons, lions and poisonous beasts we all wrestle with.

The heart is the battleground of our temptations where we win or lose those daily struggles. As such it is a place of great activity.

Jeremiah describes the heart as "devious" and "perverse" and certainly we can see those negative qualities as we are confronted by temptation and wrestle with our inner desires. We are faced with choices continually. Our greatest heart desire must be for the Lord to create within us daily a clean heart (Psalm 51:10). In turn we must be willing to work with the Holy Spirit in the process of our inner transformation.

The redemptive purpose of God in your life is to bring about transformation so that out of your heart will flow "treasures of grace". We all know the struggle this can be. We do battle daily with temptation and sin. We wrestle with the darkness of our heart and apart from God, no one knows the darkness in there better than we do ourselves. How fearful would it be to have the thoughts and intents of your heart out in the open for everyone to see.

We are continually trying to project an image, but we each know the reality. If it's any consolation, you are not alone, for we all have our struggles of the heart. At times the frustration level may seem so great that you feel like giving up. But don't!

It's in the heart where the greatest victories of life are won and issues are settled that allow you to move on in the way of the Lord. Keep your heart focused on the Lord. As Proverbs 23:17 says, "Do not let your heart envy sinners, but be zealous for the fear of the Lord all the day." Proverbs 3:5,6 tells us, "Trust in the Lord with all your heart, and lean not on your own understanding; In all your ways acknowledge Him and He shall direct your paths."

What an encouragement that is! Keep your heart focused on the Lord and you will see positive results in your life. God will lead you in the way you should go. That doesn't mean the way will be easy for there will be "rough and uneven roads" but you aren't going it alone. And as you look around you will see others on the same journey, working with the Spirit to produce hearts that please the Lord and lives that are moving together in the way of the Lord, hearts that reflect one another (Proverbs 17:19).

Think, Respond and Apply

1. Read again Makarios' word picture of the human heart. Reflect on the words and descriptions he uses to paint such a big picture. What do you learn about your own heart from these words? How does this enlarge your understanding of your heart?

2. The old adage says, "Know thyself." Do you find yourself surprised at times by what you discover in your heart, both good and bad? How well do you really know yourself?

3. Proverbs 3:5 tells you to "Trust in the Lord with all your heart, and do not rely on your own insight." What are you learning in your Christian journey about trusting in the Lord? How does it positively affect your life and bring change to your heart?

4. What are your "dragons, lions, poisonous beasts"? Focus on one you are still struggling with. Now, first, remember that the Holy Spirit is at work in you to bring about change. What can you do for your part to actively cooperate in this process of change with this one thing? Write down some clear steps you can take and begin to work through them, knowing you are not alone in this.

Pray

Often we wear a mask that allows people to see only what we want them to see. But you know your heart. You might be able to justify your actions even if they aren't what they should be, hoping you will be able to get by that way. As Proverbs 21:2 says, "Every way of a man is right in his own eyes, but the Lord weighs the hearts." You might be able to fool people but you can never fool the Lord. Pray that God will give you a heart more sensitive to the will of God for all your actions, words and thoughts. Ask the Holy Spirit to convict you where things aren't as they should be. Begin to make this a daily part of your prayers.

WEEK TWO
DAY TEN

WHAT IS MY SATISFACTION LEVEL?

Scripture For The Day
Psalm 62:5-8
My soul, wait silently for God alone, for my expectation is from Him. He only is my rock and my salvation; he is my defense; I shall not be moved. In God is my salvation and my glory; the rock of my strength, and my refuge is in God. Trust in Him at all times you people; pour out your heart before Him. God is a refuge for us.

Quote For The Day
Augustine (Sermons)
God has no need of you: but you have need of God. He seeks nothing of you, to be happy: but unless you receive it from Him, you cannot possess happiness. I do not know if you would dare to complain were you to receive from Him Who made all things something perfect which He had created. But He gives you, not something of what He has made, but Himself for your delight: He, the Creator of all things. For what of all He has made can be more perfect, more wondrous, than He who made it? 10

Reflect On This
Have you noticed how easily a child can be satisfied? For example, at Christmas a child can be overloaded with toys of all description, yet in the end may focus attention on the simplest little toy while passing over those of greater cost. A child has yet to make the same kinds of distinctions an adult does. Maybe adults should take that more into consideration when Christmas shopping.

As we grow out of childhood there are some things we take with us, never leaving them behind, and one of those relates to our satisfaction level. We may settle for dry crusts of bread when there is a feast spread before us to enjoy. You say that would never happen? Well, spiritually it happens all too often. Augustine differentiates between the better and the best in relation to what satisfies us. It's not a matter of choosing bad things. God has created so much for us to enjoy, yet, ultimately our primary choice must not focus on the gifts but on the giver, on God alone. Think about that in your own spiritual life today.

In our diet-crazed and weight conscious culture, people want things "lite". Unfortunately the concept of "lite" carries over into our spiritual nutrition and many Christians find themselves spiritually malnourished, if not on the verge of starvation. The seductive allure of our culture and all it has to promote would have us satisfied on what it offers behind the packaging of materialism, money, position, popularity, recreation and so on. These can become for us the dry crusts of bread we feed on, poor substitutes for the spiritual feast God offers us. We have to live within our culture but we don't have to buy into its value system. The more we try to satisfy our inner hunger on the "lite" menu, the lower our satisfaction level will fall and the more spiritually malnourished we will become.

Another problem related to this may be an inability to recognize spiritual nourishment when it's there. God has provided means of nourishing our souls that will leave us satisfied and we can discover rich spiritual food in worship, interaction with other Christians, a daily devotional and prayer life, Bible study and other sources of spiritual nourishment. Maybe you are trying to find satisfaction simply in that one hour of spiritual nourishment on Sunday morning while doing nothing the rest of the week. If that's your satisfaction level then you will remain spiritually malnourished.

Psalm 62, a psalm of David, is given the title, "A Calm Resolve to Wait for the Salvation of God," and that theme is evident in the words of the psalm, "My soul waits silently for God alone, for my expectation is from Him. He only is my rock and my salvation; He is my defense; I shall not be moved." Did you notice those words "alone" and "only"? "God alone...He only..." What David writes in this psalm conveys to us the level of his satisfaction. For him there is only one whom he can fully trust in for the deepest needs of his soul. No one and nothing else will do. It had to be "God alone."

The same truth is expressed in Psalm 73:25,26, "Whom have I in heaven but You? And there is none upon earth that I desire besides You. My flesh and my heart fail, but God is the strength of my heart and my portion forever." It's interesting how often this message is repeated throughout the psalms.

There is at times an almost over-powering attempt to lure us into the mindset that we can find complete satisfaction in the things of our culture which are so transitional, but the trinkets of our culture will never satisfy the hunger of your soul. God alone can do that. Don't lower your standard; if anything, raise it higher. Fads and fashions around us constantly change and even within the church culture there are so many fads and fashions that come and go. In contrast, God is the one constant, unchanging, soul-satisfying person, "God alone." Set your sights high. Find your spiritual nourishment in God and you will never go hungry and never thirst for more.

Think, Respond And Apply

1. Some diet plans recommend that you keep a diary of your daily food intake, both before you begin the diet to see what you are actually eating, as well as once you begin to see how your eating habits change. Let's make a spiritual application of this. Think about this past week and write down all the ways you fed yourself spiritually. Hold on to that list and over the coming week each time you do something to feed your spiritual life.

2. Augustine said, "I do not know if you would dare to complain were you to receive from Him Who made all things something perfect which He had created." As you consider your

spiritual life and what you have been satisfied with, how would you respond to this statement? How would the truth of this statement be evident in your life? God gives us so much good, but the good gifts are not a substitute for the Giver.

3. Take some time to think of ways you regularly feed your spiritual needs. The list can include things you listed in #1 and can go beyond that to include other things that you do. Now make a list of all the means available to you to nourish yourself spiritually-your church, Christian friends, community activities, Christian books, and any other things you can add to the list. For example, your church may offer things you have never taken advantage of. There may be a neighborhood Bible study group or some other activity you could participate in. Write them down.

4. Get alone with your Bible and journal or notebook. This may take more than one session but it will be worthwhile to follow through with it. Read through the psalms with one focus in mind: to write down all the verses you come across that speak to you of what God desires to be to you and how your life can find satisfaction in the Lord. The whole Bible is filled with many such verses, but for now keep your focus on the psalms for this exercise.

Pray

Reflect on the words of Psalm 62 in today's Scripture. Let your heart rest quietly in God's presence. Consider how God is your hope, rock, salvation, fortress and refuge. Express to God thanksgiving and praise for how He is all this to you. Express in your prayer how you want this relationship to deepen. Ask God to help you raise your satisfaction level so that you will always desire God as the one to satisfy your spiritual needs.

WEEK TWO
DAY ELEVEN

MY INNER JOURNEY

Scripture For The Day
Psalm 27:4,7-9
One thing have I desired of the Lord, that will I seek: that I may dwell in the house of the Lord all the days of my life, to behold the beauty of the Lord, and to inquire in His temple. Hear, O Lord, when I cry with my voice, have mercy also upon me, and answer me! When You said, "Seek My face," my heart said to You, "Your face, Lord, I will seek." Do not hide Your face from me; do not turn Your servant away in anger; You have been my help; do not leave me nor forsake me, O God of my salvation.

Quote For The Day
Diadochos, Bishop of Photike
    Those who meditate unceasingly upon the holy and glorious name [of Jesus] in the depths of their heart can sometimes see the radiance of their own spirit-intelligence. For when the mind is profoundly concentrated on this invocation, we feel experientially how it starts burning off all the layer of dirt that normally suffocates the soul.[11]

Reflect On This
    Do you like to travel, to venture out and see new and interesting places, meet new people and expand your horizons? Where would you really like to go? There is so much to discover in this vast world to enrich your life, not only in new countries and people but also in the magnificence of God's creation. But traveling isn't for everyone, and maybe you would be content to sit back at home and watch a travelogue on television or read a book about it.

Let's think today about taking a journey without leaving where you are, a different kind of journey, but one that can change your life. It doesn't involved going miles from where you are right now, but going within yourself.

Kallistos Ware recalls an incident from the 4th Century when Sarapion the Sindonite of Egypt, a Desert Father who liked to travel, came upon a woman in Rome who lived in one small room and never went outside. He asked her, "Why are you sitting there?" and her response was, "I am not sitting, I am on a journey."[12]

There is a connection between this incident and the expression of the psalmist David in today's Scripture. He writes, "One thing I asked of the Lord, that will I seek after: to live in the house of the Lord all the days of my life, to behold the beauty of the Lord, and to inquire in his temple." (Psalm 27:4). Now David wasn't expressing a desire to literally spend the rest of his life in the house of the Lord, but he was speaking of an inner journey to meet the Lord.

Why inward? Because the Lord has taken up residence within us; our hearts are His home. It's a matter of meeting God where He is closest to us. Today's quote speaks of "those who meditate unceasingly upon the holy and glorious Name [of Jesus] in the depths of their heart". It's a matter of moving inward to escape the outer distractions that would break our focus and concentration. But the very sense of moving inward might be a foreign concept to you. Sometimes we find silence awkward to handle and the concept of silent meditation may be foreign to your experience. We are so often conditioned to being comfortable with noise, even the background babble of a radio or television when we aren't paying attention to it. We like the "company" of noise. Adjusting to complete silence, not even hearing the sound of your own voice may be like visiting a foreign country for the first time.

David expresses God's invitation, "Seek My face!" and his response: "Your face, Lord, I will seek." (Psalm 27:8). Diadochos speaks of "those who meditate unceasingly" and "the mind is profoundly concentrated." Our familiar territory is usually outward, even in worship as we watch, listen, participate in something that unfolds outside of us. But inwardly our heart cries out to come and seek the Lord's face. Meet the Lord within your heart, in that divine sanctuary of your soul.

Does this concept make you a bit nervous or fearful? Do you fear moving too deep within yourself? It's hard to be so focused, to concentrate to such an extent when you are in unfamiliar territory, so beginning the journey may be slow. You are moving beyond the level of your external senses as you seek to commune with God within your soul, beyond the physically visible and the communication of audible words. Focus on God. Amazingly, the journey will begin to produce results in your soul. As today's quote tells us, "For when the mind is profoundly concentrated on this invocation, we feel experientially how it starts burning off all the layer of dirt that normally suffocates the soul." Inner transformation begins to take place.

We are so conditioned to think that we have to be physically doing something if we are to serve God. The concept of sitting still and being on an inward journey may be distant, that is if your sitting still in silence have always been times of daydreaming.

"Where have you been?"

"On a journey."

"That's good. Where did you go?"

"Within myself to behold the beauty of the Lord with the eyes of my soul."

Think, Respond And Apply

Are you a person who appreciates silence or does it make you a bit uncomfortable? Find a quiet place where you won't be disturbed. Read Psalm 27:4 several times. Focus your concentration on the words of the verse. Set your Bible down, close your eyes and in silence focus on the Lord. Open your mind to experience God. Write down what came to your mind and how you felt about the experience.

Did you find your mind beginning to wander? It may take several times to develop the ability to focus inwardly on the Lord in a meditative way. Precede the practice with reading a psalm or other passage of Scripture that focuses on the Lord and then pray a brief prayer of praise and worship. This should help you transition into a meditative frame of mind. Keep a record of how you progress.

Pray

In 2 Corinthians 10:5 the Apostle Paul speaks of taking "every thought captive to obey Christ." Pray that God would help you focus inwardly on Him and not allow other thoughts and images to distract you. Make Psalm 27:4 a foundation for your prayer and express your desire to God to "behold the beauty of the Lord."

SEEING MYSELF IN THE BIGGER PICTURE

Scriptures For The Day
Romans 12:3-5
For I say, through the grace given to me to everyone who is
among you, not to think of himself more highly than he ought to
think, but to think soberly, as God has dealt to each one a measure
of faith. For as we have many members in one body, but all
members do not have the same function, so we being many, are
one body in Christ, and individually members one of another.
1 Corinthians 12:12-14
For as the one body is one and has many members, but all the
members of that one body, being many, are one body, so also is
Christ. For by one Spirit we were all baptized into one body-
whether Jews or Greeks, whether slaves or free- and all have been
made to drink into one Spirit.

Quote For The Day
Aleksei Khomiakov
     No one is saved alone. He who is saved is saved in the
Church, as a member of her and in union with all her other
members. If anyone believes, he is in the communion of faith; if he
loves, he is in the communion of love; if he prays, he is in the
communion of prayer. [13]

Reflect On This
     It's a sad reality today that many professing Christians have a
take it or leave it attitude toward the Church. If they feel the
Church isn't meeting their needs, isn't living up to their
expectations, or is embroiled in controversy or division, they move
on to another or simply give up on the Church altogether. Maybe

45

you have been or are in that place. Some are on an ongoing quest to find the "perfect" local church, or a "New Testament church", not really clear about what the criteria for either would be.

The early Christians held a very high view of the church and it essential place in the life of all Christians. Cyprian of Carthage, who lived from about 200-258, wrote in his treatise "On The Unity Of The Church," in which he stressed the vital connection of the Church for all Christians, "He can no longer have God for his Father, who has not the Church for his mother."[14] In our strongly individualistic and fragmented Christian culture today, that would be a difficult statement to accept, but the fact is it is the original position from which modern churches have moved.

Can you see yourself as a Christian existing in the faith apart from the Church? As our Scripture for today tells us, by baptism the Holy Spirit places us into the body of Christ, the Church. We are members of one another. We are to view ourselves from a proper perspective, "think soberly" (Romans 12:3), understanding that we are members together, all standing equal under the grace of God and "individually members of one another." (Romans 12:5). It would seem evident from Scripture that those early Christians were right, being a member of Christ and a member of His body, the Church cannot be divided. You cannot have one without the other.

The Church is a place of spiritual birthing, nurture and growth to maturity, a place of fellowship and service. There is no perfect church. As someone has said, "The Church is not a showcase for saints but a hospital for sinners". You are part of that imperfect group, growing together on the way to perfection in Christ. It's so easy to complain about a church, a minister, the people who may rub you the wrong way, but have you ever considered how other people view you in your imperfections? No one is in the Church because they deserve to be there. It's only by God's grace and mercy that we are in Christ and in His Church.

Aleksei Khomiakov has given us a great scriptural truth, "No one is saved alone. He who is saved is saved in the Church." What a difference it can make when we view the Church from God's perspective and begin to give thanks daily for it and for the personal privilege of being part of it. It can make a very positive impact on your personal Christian life if you have an attitude of thankfulness for your church instead of one of complaining and negativity. A positive attitude will not only affect the way you view your church but it will influence how you benefit from it and how it benefits from you. You will be more open to give, both financially and through the exercise of your spiritual gifts. You will be more willing to submit to its leadership and authority in your life. You will more readily accept the Church as "the pillar and ground of the truth" (1 Timothy 2:15), instead of seeing everyone's competing opinion as being on the same level as the doctrines of the Church.

The strong individualism of today may give Christians the illusion that they can make it on their own without any connection to the Church. Such an attitude is a formula for spiritual disaster. Give God thanks for the Church and the very privilege that in Christ you are part of it.

Think, Respond And Apply

1. What part has the Orthodox Church played in your spiritual birth, nurture and development? What memories do you hold of this experience with the Church? What sense of bond does that create for you?

2. Do you find yourself at times negative and critical of the Church? Do you struggle with its problems? How can you be more constructive and supportive? What can you do to help move your local church toward positive change if that is needed? Put some thought into this and write down your conclusions.

3. Read over the quote for today. What do these words say to you and what can you learn from them?

4. Do you take advantage of the opportunities your local church community gives you to grow in your faith, develop your

gifts and in turn serve others within the Church? Think of ways you could be more effective in this.

Pray

Thank God today that you belong to Christ and in Christ belong to His Orthodox Church. Pray today for your local church, its leadership, its vision and commitment to be what God wants it to be in your community. Pray that you will become a more effective member and see yourself in the bigger picture as part of *the* One Holy Catholic and Apostolic Orthodox Church not only your local church community.

WEEK TWO
DAY THIRTEEN

PERSONAL HOLINESS

Scripture For The Day
1 Peter 1:13-16
Therefore gird up the loins of your mind, be sober, and rest your hope fully upon the grace that is to be brought to you at the revelation of Jesus Christ; as obedient children, not conforming yourselves to the former lusts , as in your ignorance; but as He who called you is holy, you also be holy in all your conduct, because it is written, "Be holy, for I am holy."

Quote For The Day
I.M. Kontzevitch (The Acquisition of the Holy Spirit)
According to the teaching of the Bible, man's "sanctity" consists of his becoming like God: the reflection and realization of divine perfection within man. Being the only bearer of the true and all-perfect, absolute life, God is also the one and only source of "sanctity". Hence, human beings may only be "participants" of His "sanctity", and this only by becoming partakers of His Divine nature. For mankind which has sinned, such sanctifying communion with God became possible only in Christ, through the power of His redeeming sacrifice. This sacrifice was the precise and perfect fulfillment of God's will for the salvation of man, that he should be holy and without blame before Him in love (Eph. 1:4). With this purpose the entire Divine Revelation concerning the salvation of man is embued.[15]

Reflect On This
How would you like your life to be viewed by your family, your friends, and your peers? Would you like to be seen as a friendly, caring, kind, accepting, interesting, patient person and

any other adjectives you can add to the list? What about putting "holy" on that list? Have you ever thought about your life in terms of being holy? We look on the saints as being holy people, famous Christian leaders, missionaries, even priests, but me? just ordinary me? It's interesting that holiness isn't usually a quality many Christians consciously strive for.

Just as the epistle of first Peter is addressed to Christians struggling to live their faith in a sometimes hostile culture, Christ calls you to live as a Christian in your world today. If holiness was an important issue for their lives maybe you need to seriously consider it for your own. It's unfortunate that often when "holy" comes to mind many people immediately think of individuals who try to give the impression of being "holier-than-thou." In reality, holiness is born out of a sense of profound humility. First Peter begins by focusing on the grace and mercy of God expressed toward sinners and our high calling in Christ. Belonging to Christ gives us hope as well as brings new meaning into our lives, meaning that relates directly to God. It gives us a new sense of identity which calls us to be consecrated to God in all our living. In Christ we are God's children. God is holy and as his children our lives are to be characterized by a practical day-to-day holiness that proclaims to others that we belong to God. Out of gratitude we live to please God in all our ways. Holiness reflects that character of God in our living and the visible reality of our spiritual transformation, "as obedient children, not conforming yourselves to the former lusts, as in your ignorance. but as He who called you is holy, you also be holy in all your conduct." (1 Peter 1:14,15).

Is holiness a relative matter, depending on a person's status or position within the Church? What should be your personal goal in holiness? It's interesting how we develop pre-conceived ideas of Christian concepts. People often relate holiness to some official ecclesial position, "Of course you have to be holy; you're a minister. That's what you get paid to be." We often set up a scale for holiness that gives the ordinary Christian a different place than that of Christian leaders. Today's quote sets forth "sanctity", or holiness as a focal part of the heritage of *every* baptized believer in Christ, through whom we become partakers of the Divine Nature. We are called to be holy because God is holy. That is for every Christian.

The standard of holiness that we find in the Bible is not the position or elevation we occupy as a Christian in the Church, but it is the holiness of God- "You shall be holy for I am holy." (1 Peter 1:16). There is no sliding scale. There is one standard of holiness for all Christians.

Holiness is not something competitive. There is no room for the attitude, "Well, I'm as good as that person," or "I'm better than a lot of people I know." Holiness is not a matter of being as good as or better in relation to other people; this is no divine contest. Holiness, in a very practical sense is the daily living expression of a life that belongs to God. Holiness relates to all of your life, not simply your church and devotional activities. We are told to "be holy in all your conduct." (1 Peter 1:15). Every activity of your life in every moment of your life is to reflect the living reality that you belong to God.

Think, Respond And Apply

1. "God is holy." What does that mean to you? What do you see in God's Person and actions that would speak to you of holiness? How does all this relate to your call as a Christian to be holy?

2. Can you think of particular Christians you know personally who would stand out to you as being holy? What makes them that way to you?

3. Read the quote for today again. It's quite apparent by what we read that holiness is a serious matter. If Christians of today took these words seriously how would it effect the Church? How would it effect the place of the church in the world?

4. Write down this statement, "If my life was to be characterized as being holy I would have to…." Reflect on what you have read today and on your life as you see it. Write down what comes to mind. Be practical and write things you see as achievable in your life.

Pray

Holiness is sometimes a difficult concept to fully understand. How do we fathom the holiness of God? How do we get around our own weaknesses and failures which we know so well to begin to see ourselves as becoming holy. Pray that God the Holy Spirit would give you a clearer vision of the holiness of God as well as a more practical understanding of how you can grow in holiness daily.

THOSE NAGGING DOUBTS

Scripture For The Day
Mark 9:20-24
Then they brought him to Him. And when he saw Him,
immediately the spirit convulsed him, and he fell on the ground
and wallowed, foaming at the mouth. So He asked his father,
"How long has this been happening to him?" And he said, "from
childhood. And often he has thrown him both into the fire and into
the water to destroy him. But if you can do anything, have
compassion on us and help us." Jesus said to him, "If you can
believe, all things are possible to him who believes." Immediately
the father of the child cried out and said with tears, "Lord, I
believe; help my unbelief!"

Quote For The Day
Bishop Kallistos Ware (The Orthodox Way)
    Because faith is not logical certainty but a personal
relationship, and because this personal relationship is as yet very
incomplete in each of us and needs continually to develop further,
it is by no means impossible for faith to coexist with doubt. The
two are not mutually exclusive. Perhaps there are some who by
God's grace retain throughout their life the faith of a little child,
enabling them to accept without question all that they have been
taught. For most of those living in the West today, however, such
an attitude is simply not possible. We have to make our own cry,
"Lord, I believe; help my unbelief" (Mark 9:24). For very many of
us this will remain our constant prayer right up to the very gates of
death. Yet doubt does not itself signify lack of faith. It may mean
the opposite- that our faith is alive and growing. For faith implies

not complacency but taking risks, not shutting ourselves off from the unknown but advancing boldly to meet it."[16]

Reflect On This

Do you wrestle with doubts, with questions that are unanswered, issues for which you cannot find a solution? If you don't then you are probably one of a very small minority, for if we are honest to ourselves and before God, we are confronted with the reality of doubt. Now that isn't always a bad thing, in fact doubt can be very positive and productive.

There is a great danger in never having questions or doubts, of accepting everything at face value and suppressing our tendency to raise questions or problems in relation to the faith. Doubt can be a challenge to go deeper in the faith, to struggle for answers, and not be satisfied with anything superficial or questionable. If your Christianity cannot stand up in the face of questions or doubts then it isn't something you can trust your life and future to.

Doubts come from one of two sources. There is the doubt of unbelief, which is seen so often from Jesus' critics in the gospels. It is in reality a skepticism that grows out of unbelief. Their questions and responses in relation to Jesus' teachings and miracles reveal an underlying heart of unbelief, to the extent that Jesus could say to them, "You are from your father the devil." (John 8:44). They weren't trying to confirm their faith in Jesus but to justify their unbelief of his claims. The other source of doubt is evident in today's Scripture, where a man whose son was possessed by an evil spirit came to Jesus seeking help. You can imagine the heartache and desperation of this father, finally coming to the place of having a glimmer of hope in this miracle-working Jesus.

The play on words between the request of the father and the response of Jesus is interesting. After telling Jesus of the boy's condition, the father added, "but if you are able to do anything, have pity on us and help us." Jesus responds in an interesting way,

54

"If you are able! All things can be done for the one who believes." Jesus focused on the issue of faith, and the father, who had come to Jesus believing He could help, recognized his lingering doubts and cried out to Jesus, "I believe; help my unbelief!" There is the acknowledgement of doubt from a heart of faith. This father knew his faith wasn't perfect, he didn't have all the answers, yet to the extent he could, he believed. His request, "help my unbelief," was serious and honest. That put him in a different category than that of Jesus' critics.

Bishop Ware, in his quote for today, shows to us the value of our doubts. They are not to be suppressed or ignored. As a matter of fact, the person who would tell you that if you are a Christian you should never have doubts can be doing great damage to your faith. Bishop Ware says "Yet doubt does not in itself signify lack of faith. It may mean the opposite- that faith is alive and growing."

There is danger in blindly believing that our faith is perfect. Christianity, which can endure our doubts and questions, will provide answers to the seeking heart. To wrestle with your doubts, to ask God the hard questions and patiently wait to discover the answers, will in the end give you a much stronger and more mature faith.

Bishop Ware gives us the challenge, "For faith implies not complacency but taking risks, not shutting ourselves off from the unknown but advancing boldly to meet it." Your faith as a Christian has to be something that can withstand the rigors of living in reality, with its pain, suffering, injustice and hardships. Lay your doubts on the table, ask the hard questions, and trust that the One who brought all things into being and knows the end from the beginning will be more than adequate to resolve those doubts and questions.

Think, Respond And Apply

1. How do you deal with your doubts and questions? Do you believe that God will think less of you if you raise them? Do

you have someone you can confide in with those doubts and questions and will help you work through them?

2. Reflect on your spiritual journey. Can you recall doubts or questions you have wrestled with in the past until you have found the answer? Are there things you still struggle with and have not discovered an adequate answer?

3. At times the Church can seem to be a very artificial environment where everyone would appear to have it all together and give no evidence of struggles or doubts. Do you have a tendency to act that way in front of other Christians, wearing a mask that would give the appearance of having it all together, without any doubt? Why would you fear removing the mask?

4. Can you see doubt as part of your spiritual learning process and a doorway to a stronger, more mature faith? Do you sometimes fear that your faith will not be able to stand up to the challenges and questions raised by the culture you live in? How will you resolve this?

Pray

Our lives are completely transparent before God, who knows out thoughts and our words even before they are spoken, according to Psalm 139:1-4. Yet God respects our freedom and will not intrude. In faith, be open to God with your doubts and questions. Lay them before God in prayer, believing that God will not be offended. Be willing to pray, "Lord, I believe; help my unbelief." If you do not already have someone, ask God to direct you to another Christian with whom you can share your doubts and struggles and who will be a help for you.

THE DISCIPLINES OF DISCIPLESHIP

Scripture For The Day
1 Timothy 4:7-10
But reject profane and old wives' fables, and exercise yourself
toward godliness. For bodily exercise profits a little but godliness
is profitable for all things, having promise of the life that now is
and of that which is to come. This is a faithful saying and worthy
of all acceptance. For to this end we both labor and suffer
reproach, because we trust in the living God, who is the Savior of
all men, especially of those who believe.

Quote For The Day
I. M. Kontzevitch (The Acquisition of the Holy Spirit)
   The way to God leads through the knowledge of oneself. "No
one can know God without knowing himself," repeats St.
Athanasius the Great after St. Anthony the Great. The knowledge
of oneself is the greatest of sciences since no one who has not
mastered it will ever know God. ... Usually, however, people
suffer from blindness and self-delusion and are unable to see their
fallen state. Therefore, becoming aware of one's own true state and
of evil within oneself is the first step towards of oneself. ... This is
a gradual process and must be accomplished in the proper order.
St. Isaac the Syrian [7th century] says: "Every virtue is the mother
of the one following it. If one should leave the mother who is
giving birth to other virtues and aspire to seek out the daughters
before attaining their mother, these virtues turn into vipers within
one's soul. If one dismisses them, one will soon die." Thus
spiritual perfection is attained gradually and in a definite order,
like building a house. On its foundation of faith one should place
the stones of obedience, endurance, abstinence, and on these- the

stones of compassion, renunciation of one's own will, etc., the cornerstones being patience and courage, which give the house its firm stability. Like a cement holding everything together, so is humility, without which not a single good deed is an act of virtue, nor is it possible to be saved. [17]

Reflect On This

As you read through the gospels you discover that Jesus was very straightforward about the cost involved in following Him. He wasn't looking for people to simply believe- He said the demons already did that- but He called people to be his disciples, to take up their cross daily and follow Him. That image is one of costly, committed following. One by one He gathered a small group of disciples who were willing to leave all and follow Him. The group grew from twelve, to seventy, to multitudes of men and women, responding to the call of Christ to be His disciples. They weren't casual bystanders, watching the "professionals" do the work of getting this new movement off the ground. They were an army of men and women and young people armed with nothing but the message of the gospel, a heart filled with the love of Christ, and a vision to change their world. Ingrained in the very fabric of the Church was a personal sense of spiritual discipline that enabled these Christians to have a singleness of focus in their lives.

The New Testament epistles are filled with encouragement and direction for spiritual formation. Disciples are called to grow in holiness and Christ-likeness and the calling isn't simply a blank sheet for us to fill in anything we may deem adequate for our development and maturity in the faith. In the Scripture for today, the Apostle Paul gives direction to Timothy by way of comparison: "Train yourself in godliness, for, while physical training is of some value, godliness is valuable in every way, holding forth the promise for both the present life and the life to come." (7,8). We constantly hear messages encouraging us to be physically fit and giving us directions to follow, both for proper nutrition as well as

58

exercise. For some reason we don't share the same concern for professing Christians who have spent years growing out of shape spiritually. Maybe you fit into that category.

The Apostle Paul points out to the Corinthian believers that they were still spiritual infants, evident by their actions, when at this stage in their spiritual journey they should be mature. We all begin our spiritual walk in a state of infancy, but God's design is for us to grow up into Christ and become mature; when we don't we find ourselves in a place of immaturity and acting like spiritual babies when we should be acting as spiritual adults.

Spiritual disciplines are designed as tools to help us effectively grow, as we are instructed in Ephesians 4:15, we must, "grow up in all things into Him who is the head- Christ." But we aren't robots, we aren't programmed to automatically do this. You have to understand your purpose in Christ and make the commitment and concentrated effort to use the tools at hand to grow. It's a day-by-day, step-by-step progression. It may seem slow at times and you may falter and even slip back at times, but God has promised to enable you to continue on the path.

Over the next few days you will be introduced to several spiritual disciplines, certainly not an exhaustive list, but some will be familiar and some may be new to you. They are all tools God gives you to effectively become the Christ-centered person you are designed to be. Again you need to be reminded that you are not alone. You have the Church, the Body of Christ to help and support you and you also have the Holy Spirit to empower you and direct you on the path. Don't lose heart, take it one day at a time. See the disciplines as a source of blessing and you will be richly rewarded for the effort you put forth.

Think, Respond And Apply

1. The comparison in today's Scripture between physical training and spiritual training is a valid one made for a practical purpose. When you stop and consider your physical needs and then

reflect on your spiritual needs, how do you respond to this comparison? What does it say to you personally?

2. Have you ever been involved in something that took a great deal of personal discipline and commitment- maybe involvement in a sport or striving to earn a degree, or something else? At the time how did you accept the need for discipline and the price you were being called to pay to achieve your desired goal? Looking back, was it worth the effort? Is being a faithful disciple of Jesus Christ a goal any less worthy of your focused discipline?

3. During his earthly ministry Jesus would easily fit into the leadership mantra, "Lead by example!" When you consider the ministry of Jesus in the gospels, where do you see discipline in His life and what can you learn from His example?

4. Do you have time for some extra reading? Here are some books for your consideration: *The Philokalia* (four volumes of wise spiritual direction), *Turning the Heart to God*, by St. Theophan the Recluse, *Counsels From the Holy Mountain* by Elder Ephriam and *The Mystery of the Church* by William Bush.*

Pray

If you have come this far in the book you are serious about your spiritual life and its healthy development. Give thanks to God for all the resources you have at your disposal to become all that God wants you to be. Pray that God will give you the desire for a disciplined heart to follow after Christ. Pray that the Holy Spirit would empower and direct you on this journey as it deepens. Be open with God about your struggles and fears in this journey.

*(Available from Regina Orthodox Press)

WEEK THREE
DAY SIXTEEN

PRAYER-A HEART IN TUNE TO GOD

Scripture For The Day
Matthew 6:9-13
In this manner, therefore, pray: Our Father in heaven, hallowed be
Your name. Your kingdom come. Your will be done, on earth as it
is in heaven. Give us this day our daily bread. And forgive us our
debts, as we forgive our debtors. And do not lead us into
temptation, but deliver us from the evil one. For Yours is the
kingdom and the power and the glory forever. Amen

Quote For The Day
Evagrios the Solitary (On Prayer)
   Do not pray for the fulfillment of your wishes, for they may
not accord with the will of God. But pray as you have been taught
saying: Thy will be done in me (cf. Luke 22:42). Always entreat
Him in this way- that His will be done. For He desires what is
good and profitable for you, whereas you do not always ask for
this. Often when I have prayed I have asked for what I thought was
good, and persisted in my petition, stupidly importuning the will of
God, and not leaving it to Him to arrange things as He knows is
best for me. But when I have obtained what I have asked for, I
have been very sorry that I did not ask for the will of God to be
done; because the thing turned out not to be as I had thought.[18]

Reflect On This
   The practice of prayer permeates the Bible from Genesis to
Revelation and in those pages we discover the prayers of the
patriarchs, prophets, psalmists, apostles, sinners, and ultimately of
Jesus Christ himself. It is evident by its use in Scripture that prayer
plays a significant role in the life of a follower of God. Yet, if we

are honest, we would often have to admit the difficulty of maintaining a consistent, meaningful prayer life. It doesn't come easy and often involves personal struggle. We must come to see prayer as a spiritual discipline of the soul and necessary for our spiritual wellbeing.

Prayer was a priority of Jesus during His earthly ministry. Often we find Him escaping from the crowds to a solitary place to commune with His heavenly Father. He acknowledges His dependence on the Father and gives thanks in the working of His miracles. In the garden before His betrayal and trial He agonized in prayer over what was before Him. Even from the cross He cried out to the Father. Now if the One Who was on this earth as God incarnate expressed by His personal practice the importance of prayer, how much more should we pray who are so well aware of our sins, weaknesses and needs, as well as our gratitude to a merciful, loving God?

Today's quote isn't an expression of sentimental idealism, but in a very real sense opens our minds to the true activity of prayer. To stop and reflect on what prayer is and who it is we are communicating to should give us this same sense. We can communicate with the Lord God Almighty! Jesus encourages us to come before God, praying in the name of Jesus Christ, and God will hear our prayers, regardless of what we may feel about our personal insignificance. Within the biblical framework of existence and understanding, we live before a personal Creator-Redeemer God who not only understands us, but seeks communication from us. God has communicated with us in the ultimate sense in Jesus Christ and the writer of the book of Hebrews (4:14,16) encourages us, "Seeing then that we have a great High Priest who has passed through the heavens, Jesus, the Son of God, let us hold fast our confession.... Let us therefore come boldly to the throne of grace, that we may obtain mercy and find grace to help in time of need." There is your personal invitation.

Prayer can become a monotonous, short-lived exercise if it has no purpose and balance. Jesus gave instruction in prayer in those familiar words we have come to know as "The Lord's Prayer." It is brief, concise prayer that expresses what prayer should be. Unfortunately, when prayer is thought of simply as a personal wish list of our wants and needs then it will never be seen in its importance as a spiritual discipline. God does answer prayer and meet our needs, but if we simply look to God as some heavenly Santa Claus who exists simply to fill our daily wish list then we are misusing prayer.

When you reflect on the Lord's Prayer you discover the essential components of prayer, expressed in the familiar acronym-ACTS- Adoration, Confession, Thanksgiving and Supplication. Our daily prayers should be a balanced expression of worship, confession of our sins, thanksgiving for all God provides, as well as the presentation of our needs and the needs of others we pray for. Prayer is a spiritual discipline that you can be growing in daily through your waking hours.

We are called in 1 Thessalonians 5:17 to "pray without ceasing." Your response right now may be that you find it difficult to pray for five minutes a day, so how could you ever do that? Again, think of prayer as a discipline. It takes time, practice and work to develop. In recent years we have been told about the value of specific prayers, like "the prayer of Jabez," which has spawned a whole mini-industry of things related to this prayer. Yet centuries before someone came upon the prayer of Jabez, the Orthodox Church, emphasized the unceasing use of "The Jesus Prayer"- "Lord Jesus Christ, Son of God, have mercy on me a sinner."

One of the most inspirational and spiritually powerful books on this prayer is a little book translated from the Russian, called *The Way Of A Pilgrim*. Prayerfully read it and come to understand the centuries-old importance of this simple prayer. Ultimately, may the expression of your heart be that of the early disciples, "Lord, teach me to pray."

Think, Respond And Apply
	1. Reflect on the present condition of your prayer life and seriously evaluate it. How meaningful is it to you? Where are you struggling with it and why? After considering what you have read today, do you see ways your prayer life must change? Be specific.
	2. St John of Kronstadt wrote, "Prayer is a state of continual gratitude." Would gratitude characterize your praying? Consider intentionally adding to every prayer at least one specific expression of gratitude to God. See what a difference it will make.
	3. Does your local church emphasize prayer as a spiritual discipline and encourage its corporate and personal practice? Become vocal and enthusiastic about enlarging the place of prayer in your local church Ask God for direction in this. Talk to your priest about it.
	4. Have you ever considered having a prayer partner, someone with whom you could develop a mutual ministry of prayer? Have you got a good book of Orthodox prayers? If not get one and begin to use it every day. *Orthodox Prayers For Every Day* is an excellent prayer book for personal use.*

Pray
	On a piece of paper write down the four words mentioned today- Adoration, Confession, Thanksgiving, Supplication. Beside each word write specific things that come to your mind as matters of prayer. Now bring these things to God in prayer, and as well, ask God to enable you to grow in this important spiritual discipline.

*(Available from Regina Orthodox Press)

WEEK THREE
DAY SEVENTEEN

MEDITATION AND SCRIPTURE

Scripture For The Day
Psalm 119:9-16
How can a young man cleanse his way? By taking heed according
to Your word. With my whole heart have I sought You; Oh, let me
not wander from Your commandments! Your word have I hidden
in my heart, That I might not sin against You. Blessed are You, O
Lord! Teach me Your statutes. With my lips I have declared all the
judgments of Your mouth. I have rejoiced in the way of Your
testimonies, As much as in all riches. I will meditate on Your
precepts, And contemplate Your ways. I will delight myself in
Your statutes; I will not forget Your word.

Quote For The Day
St. Mark the Ascetic (On Spiritual Law)
 When reading the Holy Scriptures, he who is humble and
engaged in spiritual work will apply everything to himself and not
to someone else. Call upon God to open the eyes of your heart, so
that you may see the value of prayer and spiritual reading when
understood and applied. Understand the words of Holy Scripture
by putting them into practice, and do not fill yourself with conceit
by expatiating [wandering off into] on theoretical ideas. He who
neglects action and depends on theoretical knowledge holds a staff
of reed instead of a double-edged sword; and when he confronts
his enemies in time of war, 'it will go into his hand, and pierce it'
(2 Kings 18:21), injecting its natural poison. [19]

Reflect On This
 It is interesting that the longest chapter in the Bible focuses
our attention on the place of Scripture in our lives and how it is to

have an overall impact on our whole being. We are to think on it, meditate on it, hide it in our hearts, until it becomes part of the very fabric of our being. Meditation calls us to go deeper, moving beyond a quick read as we rush through our day.

Maybe you have the experience of trying to grab a few minutes of Bible reading as you begin or end your day. You discover the early morning lingering mental fog from your night's sleep or the late evening mental slowdown in preparation for sleep limits the benefit you receive from your reading.

Sometimes we strive to read through the Bible in a year, a commendable practice, or have times when we read as much as we can at one sitting. Meditation calls us to slow down and go deeper, to focus your mind on a single verse or phrase, or even just a word; to let the Scripture sink deep into your mind to the point that it becomes part of your subconscious, part of you. It isn't gone five minutes after you return to your daily activities. As you read in today's quote, "Call upon God to open the eyes of your heart, so that you may see the value of prayer and spiritual reading when understood and applied." The purpose of our meditation should be transformation- transforming your knowledge of God, your knowledge of yourself, transformation of your very life. It is evident in Psalm 119 that the impact of Scripture was to be life-changing and life-long, but not instant. Meditation speaks to us of a day-by-day progression in our personal transformation through this life-long practice.

Time is not our enemy. We all have the same amount of it, but how we manage that time and order our priorities is critical. If spiritual transformation is a priority for your life then ordering your priorities within the time frame of your days is essential. Meditation requires time, quiet time, not simply in relation to surrounding distractions, but quiet in terms of your mental and emotional distractions as well. The latter may be the most difficult to deal with.

Quiet your heart and mind before God. Ask for divine assistance to help you focus. Be still before God. Let the verse, the phrase, the word, become the center of your focus. This isn't a Bible study time. It's a time to let the Scripture settle and saturate your mind with the depth of its meaning and to let God speak to you through it. Let the Bible do its work. It may touch you mentally, emotionally, spiritually, but don't attempt to force it to a conclusion or rush it along. Something is happening within you and you may struggle with the fact that you are not in control of this or orchestrating the outcome. God is at work.

Meditation, as with any spiritual discipline, will take time to develop. Often our minds are wild and restless, overburdened to the point we find it hard to come down to a single focus. Prayer, discipline and practice will help. Day by day it will become more familiar and somewhat easier, although the challenges will always be there. But the rewards are worth it as transformation begins to take place. The mind focused on and saturated with Scripture becomes a mind saturated with God and in turn produces a life that reflects God and the reality of God within.

Think, Respond And Apply

1. Do you have a daily time to read the Bible and reflect on what you read? How successful and beneficial do you find this practice? What problems do you encounter?

2. St. Mark the Ascetic says, "When reading the Holy Scriptures, he who is humble and engaged in spiritual work will apply everything to himself and not to someone else." How much personal application do you receive from your Bible reading? Can you see how meditation- "spiritual work"- would make a positive improvement in this? Meditation should not replace your Bible reading but be in addition to it because the two are different.

3. Are you a person who is concerned about always being in control of your life? Meditation in a very real sense is an activity in which you relinquish that control to the particular Scripture of

your focus and to the Spirit of God who is at work in your life to bring about change. How do you feel about that? What particular concerns may you have about it?

    4. As you have considered the spiritual discipline of meditation on Scripture today, other factors may have entered into the picture; for example the issue of time and personal priorities. Examine your days and your schedule and intentionally block out personal time for meditation. Make sure you give yourself time and space as free from distraction as possible. Do some spiritual time management.

Pray

    Change doesn't always come easily and sometimes it begins with a slow, stumbling attempt. If you are entering into this spiritual discipline of meditation for the first time it will be a challenge, but you are not alone in this. Pray that God will give you a clear sense of the importance of this discipline, the ability to so order your time that you have adequate room for it in your day, as well as inner strength to discipline your mind in this process.

WEEK THREE
DAY EIGHTEEN

THE SPIRITUAL INTIMACY OF WORSHIP

Scripture For The Day
Psalm 113:1-3
Praise the Lord! Praise, O servants of the Lord, praise the name of
the Lord! Blessed be the name of the Lord from this time on and
forevermore! From the rising of the sun to its going down the
Lord's name is to be praised.

Quote For The Day
     Praying With The Orthodox Tradition
     A Morning Prayer:
O Lord our God, You enabled us to cast drowsiness aside and in
calling us to a holy life You brought us to lift our hands to You at
midnight to worship you in thanksgiving for Your righteous laws;
so hear now our prayers and supplications: accept our grateful
confession of faith and our night-time offering of praise. Give us
freely, O God, a firm faith, unfailing hope and heartfelt love; bless
us in our going out and coming in, and in all we do or say or wish
for. Grant that we may await the break of day with songs of praise,
worship and adoration as we bless Your goodness and
indescribable power. For Your most holy Name is to be celebrated
in hymns of blessing and Your majesty is to be glorified, Father,
Son and Holy Spirit, now and forever, to the ages of ages. Amen.
[20]

Reflect On This
     Have you ever stepped outside on a clear, cloudless night and
looked up into the sky at the vast expanse of space in all its beauty,
the stars, the planets, the constellations? Has such a scene ever left
you with an overwhelming sense of awe and the urge to break out

in praise and worship of the God Who brought it all into being? Our minds too often get fixed on worship as a corporate liturgical experience in a certain place, under certain conditions, with certain components. Worship certainly centers on the Liturgy within our Orthodox communities. But we also discover that those who worship God corporately, within the temple or the Church *also* worship God personally. The psalms are filled with personal worship and serve as a good guide for developing your own discipline of worship.

There is a distinction between your personal devotions, times of Bible study, times of meditation and a time of personal worship, although worship could be incorporated in any of these other times with God or flow from them. Worship, going back to the root of the word, is giving God worth, ascribing to God praise and glory, exalting God with blessing and rejoicing. It moves beyond prayer, beyond Bible reading and study, to unleash the flood of praise and rejoicing from your heart and soul. It can be stirred by a passage of Scripture, like that of Psalm 113, or from the awesome glory of God's creation that may take your breath away and thrill your soul, or even as a response to something God has done in your life. It can be a very spontaneous experience that can take place any time, any where- in a crowd of people where you may silently lift up your heart to God in worship, or on a solitary hillside as you take in the vast expanse of a beautiful creation.

Worship demands a heart in tune to God, even for Liturgical communal worship on a Sunday morning, or else you become simply a spectator to what is unfolding- and worship can never be a spectator experience. The fullness of worship unfolds in sounds, sights, smells, tastes, touch- all your senses. They may not all be engaged in every experience of worship, but they all will be at some time. Whatever the situation of worship, there must be a heart in tune with God, or you will simply be going through the motions, even in church, and your heart and soul will be still.

We often think of a building, a specific place as a sanctuary for worship, and certainly it is. It's a holy space where you come to meet God in the midst of the Church. As you begin to understand all of creation in relation to God, you come to realize that anywhere can be a holy place where you can encounter God and respond in worship.

The basis of all true worship is the Liturgy. However we carry that spirit of the Liturgy into every part of life and every place. There is a need to develop that sense of God's Being and Presence in your daily living. Where I am God is. Where God is I can worship. There are no time and space constraints. If David could worship God on the solitary hillsides of Israel and Paul and Silas could worship God in a Philippian jail in the middle of the night, you can worship God wherever you are. The issue is not time and place but the condition of your heart, a heart in tune to worshiping God. And a heart so in tune to God would never say, "I don't need to go to church to worship; I can worship God alone." It's never an either/or situation, unless physical infirmity prevents you from going to church to worship.

The Orthodox prayer that makes up today's quote is a daily prayer to be prayed at dawn, a beautiful invocation to God, devoting the day to worship. "Grant that we may await the break of day with songs of praise, worship and adoration as we bless your goodness and indescribable power." Worship is not meant to be a one hour a week experience. If that is all it is to you, it will never play a major role in your life and that's sad for any professing Christian. Worship is a spiritual discipline to be developed daily in your life as you live in the fullness of God's presence, as much as can be experienced this side of heaven, and your worship gives you a small taste of Heaven before you arrive.

Think, Respond And Apply

1. Have you ever had a spontaneous worship moment, a time when something just overwhelmed you with a sense of God

71

and filled you with a response of praise and adoration toward God? Maybe it has happened more than once in the Liturgy or outside of it, but describe one experience and the impact it had on you.

2. When you are worshipping within a church in the Liturgy do you sometimes feel like a spectator to all that is happening and not a participant in the worship? Why do you think this happens?

3. Do you believe that daily worship is an important part of your life? Why? If it is, how does it impact your life, or if it isn't yet, how do you think it would affect your life?

4. What steps can you take to develop the daily discipline of worship in a way that it will become a normal daily spiritual discipline and reinforce your worship in church on Sunday?

Pray

Pray today that God would enlarge your vision of worship so that you could respond more daily in spontaneous worship of God, as well as enter into the fullness of worship within the Church (congregation) on Sunday. Pray that God would give you a heart that would overflow in gratitude and praise daily.

FASTING TO HUNGER FOR GOD

Scriptures For The Day
Matthew 6:16-18
Moreover, when you fast, do not be like the hypocrites with a sad
countenance. For they disfigure their faces that they may appear to
men to be fasting. Assuredly I say to you, they have their reward.
But you, when you fast, anoint your head and wash your face, so
that you do not appear to men to be fasting, but to your Father who
is in the secret place; and your Father who sees in secret will
reward you openly.
Matthew 9:14-17
Then the disciples of John came to Him, saying, "Why do we and
the Pharisees fast often, but your disciples do not fast?" And Jesus
said to them, "Can the friends of the bridegroom mourn as long as
the bridegroom is with them? But the days will come when the
bridegroom will be taken away from them, and then they will fast.
No one puts a piece of unshrunk cloth on an old garment; for the
patch pulls away from the garment, and the tear is made worse.
Nor do they put new wine into old wineskins, or else the wineskins
break, the wine is spilled, and the wineskins are ruined. But they
put new wine into new wineskins, and both are preserved."

Quote For The Day
Kallistos Ware (The Orthodox Way)
Knowing that man is not an angel but a unity of body and soul, the
Orthodox Church insists upon the spiritual value of bodily fasting.
We do not fast because there is anything in itself unclean about the
act of eating and drinking. Food and drink are, on the contrary,
God's gift, from which we are to partake with enjoyment and
gratitude. We fast, not because we despise the divine gift, but so as

73

to make ourselves aware that it is indeed a gift- so as to purify our eating and drinking, and to make them, no longer a concession to greed, but a sacrament and a means of communion with the Giver. Understood in this way, ascetic fasting is directed not against the body but against the flesh [The term "flesh"...signifies whatever within us is sinful and opposed to God]. Its aim is not destructively to weaken the body, but creatively to render the body more spiritual. [21]

Reflect On This

Does food play a major role in your life? Most Christians in North America know very little of physical hunger. We seem to have an abundance of food and medical statistics tell us that we are often eating too much and the medical system is overworked with medical problems relating to overeating. It's a common problem in our society in contrast with much of the rest of the world.

Even in Orthodox circles food plays a role in what we do together, from coffee and donuts to church suppers. Food and fellowship seem to have a close relationship. So when the topic of fasting is introduced, we may struggle to make it a personal part of our worship and observance of the fast days of the Church.

One of the accusations brought against Jesus, as we see in the Scripture for today, was that he and his disciples did not keep the traditional fasts. Jesus' response was that there would be a time for fasting once He was gone, yet it would not be the legalistic fasting of His day that was so often done for appearance sake. In Matthew 6:16-18, Jesus instructed that fasting was not to be done in a hypocritical way simply for appearance, but as a private spiritual exercise before God, "so that your fasting may be seen not by others but by your Father who is in secret; and your Father who sees in secret will reward you."

As we read the Book of Acts we discover that the Church practiced fasting and often fasting went together with prayer and was used in preparation to making important decisions (Acts

13:2,3; 14:23). It is evident that the practice of fasting continued in the Church because in the early centuries of the Church fasting had become a regular part of the church life, both corporate fasting at times like Advent and Lent, as well as personal fasting as a spiritual discipline. There is much written on fasting by the early leaders of the Church. Saint Chrysostom, one of the Church Fathers, said of fasting, "That you may learn how great a good is fasting and how effective a shield against the devil, and also, that after receiving baptism it behooves us not to incline towards pleasure, but towards mortification. He (Jesus) fasted; not because He needed to, but to teach us. And that He may lay down the length of our Lenten fast, He fasted for forty days and forty nights." [22]

For some unfortunate reason, the spiritual discipline of fasting, both personally and corporately, has disappeared from much of the Protestant church. Yet still today within the Orthodox Church fasting plays an integral role in our worship and personal spiritual development.

You can fast to lose weight. You can fast to cleanse your body internally and improve your health. You can fast for any number of good reasons, but fasting as a spiritual discipline must focus on God. Fasting, as the quote for today explains, is for the purpose of purifying the passions, denying that which in itself is good- food, for what is best- God, and in so doing, you make a sacrifice to become more focused on God.

How much do you hunger for God? Enough to deny your physical appetites, to set them aside for a time and focus all your energy on your spiritual hunger? Again this is a matter of spiritual discipline. At what price am I willing to set aside my physical needs to bring my soul under the discipline and experience of God? On a larger scale, in the Church Year, both Advent and Lent are times of spiritual preparation and fasting plays an important role in that preparation, denying that which is, in and of itself, good, in order to focus on the best- to prepare our hearts for God in prayer, repentance, confession and worship.

Christians are called to practice a corporate fast for a spiritual purpose. Sadly for many today, this practice is ignored or rejected as an unnecessary legalistic imposition, and our souls are impoverished by such neglect.

Fasting is an important spiritual discipline for all Christians and if you are just beginning in it you may be struck by, not what you are giving up, but by all you gain in return. The spiritual rewards can be many.

Think, Respond And Apply

1. What has been your view of fasting up to today? What do you think has shaped your attitude and thoughts toward it?

2. Fasting does not necessarily involve just food. You can also fast from other things in your life in order to devote yourself to God and your spiritual development. What in your life could you fast from for a time in order to devote yourself more intensely to God?

3. Fasting as a spiritual discipline has a common bond with all spiritual disciplines- it is a discipline, and as such will demand your attention, commitment and determination. What concerns or fears do you have about fasting and if you presently don't practice it, what would hold you back from adding this spiritual discipline from your life?

4. The Church calendar has long periods of fasting at Advent and Lent, removing certain foods from the diet. As well, Wednesdays and Fridays are regular fast days as instructed by the Church, but not with a total fast from all food. But a personal spiritual discipline should begin small, one step at a time. Ask your priest to advise you. Then consider setting a day aside for a personal fast. If you have no serious health problems that might be affected, plan a day-long fast. Just consume liquids for the day and use the time you would usually be preparing and eating meals to

prepare and take in spiritual nourishment. Include prayer, Scripture reading, reading from a devotional writing, and a time for personal introspection and meditation. Keep a journal of your day and the benefit you receive from it. You may also consider using the money you saved on those meals to give to a food bank or a local organization helping with poverty. If you are not already doing so, consider participating in the regular Orthodox Church fast days.

Pray
    God gives us all things to enjoy, including food and nourishment for our bodies and we need to be thankful for it all. Spend time in prayer giving God thanks, but at the same time expressing your heart's desire for God, above all the provisions you receive. The discipline of fasting begins with the discipline of prayer in expressing your need and seeking God's help.

THE DISCIPLINE OF DAILY REPENTANCE

Scriptures For The Day
Acts 2:37,38
Now when they heard this, they were cut to the heart and said to
Peter and the rest of the apostles, "Men and brethren, what shall we
do?" Then Peter said to them, "Repent, and let every one of you be
baptized in the name of Jesus Christ for the remission of sins; and
you shall receive the gift of the Holy Spirit."
2 Corinthians 7:9,10
Now I rejoice, not that you were made sorry, but that your sorrow
led to repentance. For you were made sorry in a godly manner, that
you might suffer loss from us in nothing. For godly grief produces
repentance leading, to salvation, not to be regretted; but the sorrow
of the world produces death.

Quote For The Day
Stelios Ramfos (Like A Pelican In The Wilderness)
   Repentance is a change at the center of one's desire. What is
important is not so much the scale of the transgression as the
intensity and depth of the inward change of heart.... the attainment
of repentance reflects a practical concern for freedom, the freedom
to do the will of God. [23]

Reflect On This
   On the day of Pentecost, in response to the Apostle Peter's
sermon, the question was asked, "Brothers, what should we do?"
Peter responded with these words, "Repent and let every one of
you be baptized in the name of Jesus Christ for the remission of
sins; and you shall receive the gift of the Holy Spirit." (Acts
2:37,38). In Protestant churches often repentance is viewed only in

relation to conversion, a one-time action that need not be repeated. But as you look into Scripture, both the Old and New Testaments speak of repentance as an ongoing activity in the life of a believer. The term "repentance" basically means a change of mind. We all know ourselves well enough, if we are honest, to know that our minds need to be changed continuously, especially when it comes to our sins and our relationship with God.

Today's quote tells us, "Repentance is a change at the center of one's desire." It is a heart change which must be an ongoing, life-long process. Therefore we must come to view repentance as a spiritual discipline which must be practiced daily. The biblical concept of repentance has both a negative and positive aspect, in saying "NO" to sin and "YES" to God.

We see that twofold aspect in response to the sermon in Acts: turn from, turn toward. We see it as well in the repentance of the Corinthian believers in today's Scripture. They were grieved when brought face-to-face with their sins, but it didn't stop there, because, "Your sorrow led to repentance; for you were made sorry in a godly manner." It goes on to say, "For godly sorrow produces a repentance leading to salvation, not to be regretted."

The struggle with sin is ongoing in our lives. We are well aware of our sins and our failures. They are not small matters with God, but need to be acknowledged and turned from, or they become impediments to us becoming what God desires us to be. As today's quote tells us, "the attainment of repentance reflects a practical concern for freedom, the freedom to do the will of God."

It may be that your concept of repentance is that of a dark, negative, introspective brooding over sins and failures. In contrast, biblically, repentance is seen as a daily turning to God, a daily saying "Yes" to God in acknowledging divine mercy and grace at work in your heart. God doesn't call you to dwell on your failures and inabilities, but to turn daily to the resources of divine ability and mercy. Repentance is an important part of focusing your life on God continually and turning from that which would entice you away from your God-centeredness.

The positive aspect of repentance is stressed in these words of Bishop Kallistos Ware, "Correctly understood, repentance is not negative but positive. It means not self-pity or remorse but conversion, the re-centering of our whole life upon the Trinity... It is to see, not what we failed to be, but what by divine grace we can now become; and it is to act upon what we see. To repent is to open our eyes to the light. Repentance is not just a single act, an initial step, but a continuing state, an attitude of heart and will that needs to be ceaselessly renewed up to the end of life." [24]

Repentance as a spiritual discipline is a daily affirmation that by the grace of God you desire to move on in holiness and Christ-likeness. You want to remove any hindrance from achieving that goal. It is an open acknowledgement of your personal need and a plea for divine help to keep turning toward God. At times the process can be painful and difficult, and as our Scripture today said, may cause grief, but that grief is quickly turned to joy and hope in the Lord as your life is freed from the unneeded baggage of sin and failure. As the writer of the epistle of Hebrews encourages us, "Let us lay aside every weight and the sin which so easily ensnares us, and let us run with endurance the race that is set before us." (Hebrews 12:1).

In the disciplined process of becoming a Christ-like disciple, will you find repentance to be a valued tool as it works deep in your soul.

Think, Respond And Apply

1. A statement in today's quote describes one result of the work of repentance as "the freedom to do the will of God." Do you find yourself free to do God's will? If not, what hindrances do you struggle with and how would repentance help you?

80

2. The Apostle Paul links together grief and repentance. Do you ever find yourself grieving over your sins and your failures? Does it ever bring a sense of despair into your life?

3. What place has the discipline of repentance played in your life up to this point? Do you see any difference between the call to confess your sins and the call to repent? Sin in Scripture is always viewed in a negative sense. What is the positive effect of repentance from the heart?

4. Take some quiet time to do some serious introspection. Think on those things in your life that may be hindering you in your freedom to do the will of God and live in the fullness of the joy of the Lord. Write down those things that are having a negative effect, sins, failures, whatever they may be, and one by one decide to deal with them and cut the chains that hold you back. Talk to your priest. Make time with him to go to confession.

Pray

Pray that God would give you an introspective heart, that under the direction of the Holy Spirit you would allow repentance to do its work and give you the freedom to do God's will daily. Pray that the Lord will help you to make a good confession to your priest and help you to develop a close and trusting relationship with him (or with your spiritual father, if your confessor is some other priest).

WEEK THREE
DAY TWENTY-ONE

DISCIPLINED RESULTS: SEEING JESUS IN YOUR MIRROR

Scripture For The Day
2 Corinthians 3:17,18
Now the Lord is the Spirit; and where the Spirit of the Lord is, there is liberty. But we all, with unveiled faces, beholding as in a mirror the glory of the Lord, are being transformed into the same image from glory to glory; just as by the Spirit of the Lord.

Quote For the Day
Stelios Ramfos (Like A Pelican In The Wilderness)
    The path of grace is not mapped out in an objective way for us to seek it through well-ordered arrangements. It passes through the seat of our interior cauterization. Such fire may burn us; it can however, if we wish it, consume all our rust, destroy everything that rots us. Just as God does not violate our freedom, so His grace takes our identity into consideration. The lack of a sense of our own identity is the biggest obstacle that we can put in the path of grace. Let us reflect on this: The new life has to be made our own. This means that our salvation rests on our personal uniqueness, on an actual freedom which results in our not having anyone exactly like us.... We see the face of God only with our own individual eyes. 25

Reflect On This
    What do you see when you look in the mirror? Do you notice another wrinkle or maybe a bit more gray hair? Maybe you like what you see; the view is improving. One thing for sure, what you see in the mirror is one of a kind. There is only one you, in all your uniqueness, not just in what you see in your face, but in your

82

whole being. You are not an accident but a definite creation by God.

Sometimes the fact is overlooked that in re-creating us in Christ, God preserves our individual uniqueness, personality, emotional makeup, who we are as persons. Spiritual development isn't a "cookie cutter" process, turning out identical Christians. God is in the process of re-creating us in the image of Christ, but as the persons we are, not as clones.

In the process of growing through the spiritual disciplines this is an important fact to remember. The spiritual disciplines are used by God to mold you into the image of Christ within the framework of your individual person. God isn't interested in obliterating your personality, or any aspect of your individual uniqueness you were born with. Along with those birth traits, there are also cultural and ethnic traits that remain with you for life and are neutral matters in becoming like Christ. Those things will remain.

The disciplined growth under the Holy Spirit's direction will deal with matters that reflect upon your fallenness, your sinfulness and the resulting weaknesses. The Holy Spirit builds within your life the spiritual fruit that is mentioned in Galatians 5:22,23, which reflects the character of Christ. The spiritual disciplines focus your life on Christ daily.

Day by day, step by step, a transformation process is unfolding in your life. It may not happen as fast as you would like. There may be setbacks at times. But if you have a disciplined commitment to this path, you can be sure the results will appear- "But we all with unveiled face, beholding as in a mirror the glory of the Lord; are being transformed into the same image from glory to glory..." The Apostle Paul encouraged the Corinthian Christians to "Imitate me, just as I also imitate Christ." (1 Corinthians 11:1). He wasn't interested in creating a church full of little Saint Pauls, but he was very interested in creating a church full of little Christs, to have all those believers model Jesus Christ in their lives. You may have a mature Christian you hold in high esteem and desire to imitate, but don't try to become a copy of that person, but to become a copy of Jesus Christ as modeled in that person. That is your challenge.

As today's quote challenges you, "The new life has to be made our own. This means that our salvation rests on our personal uniqueness, on an actual freedom which results in our not having anyone exactly like us...." Don't turn your back on who you are as a person, for such a reaction reflects on God who made you. Open your eyes to see that through the path of spiritual discipline your unique person can be transformed into a Christ-like uniqueness. Don't look to the person next to you to see if you are identical to them, but look to Christ to see if you are identical to Him in those spiritual qualities that reflect the character of God.

You can't have someone else's experience. Your pilgrimage will be your own, as unique as you are, because that is how God deals with us. Don't seek some else's experience but walk the path God has laid out for you. Seek advice and counsel, follow your spiritual leaders and seek to imitate their Christ-like qualities, but always remember, as today's quote states, "We see the face of God with our own individual eyes."

Think, Respond And Apply

1. What do you like about yourself- your personality, your emotional makeup, even those aspects of your cultural/ethnic identity? As you reflect on these things, how does this positive reflection cause you to feel about yourself? Do you struggle with self-acceptance?

2. Our fallenness impacts our personal being in different ways. Look at yourself through this lens now and reflect upon what you would like to see change through the exercise of spiritual disciplines and the work of the Holy Spirit. What kind of positive impact would these changes make in your life?

3. Do you know a mature Orthodox Christian whom you respect and look up to? What do they model in their life that you would like to have in yours?

4. Today's quote begins, "The path of grace is not mapped out in an objective way for us to seek it through well-ordered arrangements." You may find Christians who would give you the impression that spiritual maturity can be attained through four or five easy steps. Experience will teach you the truth of the quote. Do you find your spiritual past sometimes like a maze? What discourages and frustrates you on your journey? What has encouraged you recently?

Pray

Psalm 139:14 says, "I will praise You for I am fearfully and wonderfully made." Celebrate your uniqueness before God and give thanks that God has created you as the person you are. If you struggle with self-acceptance be honest with God about this. Ask God to enable you to see the uniqueness of your spiritual pilgrimage and encourage you on your disciplined path to Christlikeness.

HUMILITY, A HEART FITTED FOR SERVICE

Scripture For The Day
John 13:1-5, 12-17
Now before the Feast of the Passover, when Jesus knew that His hour had come that He should depart from this world to the Father, having loved His own who were in the world, He loved them to the end. And supper being ended, the devil having already put into the heart of Judas Iscariot, Simon's son, to betray Him, Jesus, knowing that the Father had given all things into His hands, and that He had come from God and was going to God, rose from supper and laid aside His garments, took a towel and girded Himself. After that, he poured water into a basin and began to wash the disciples' feet, and to wipe them with the towel with which He was girded . . . So when He had washed their feet, taken His garments, and sat down again, He said to them, "Do you know what I have done to you? You call me Teacher and Lord, and you say well, for so I am. If I then, your Lord and Teacher, have washed your feet, you also ought to wash one another's feet. For I have given you an example, that you should do as I have done to you. Most assuredly, I say to you, a servant is not greater than his master; nor is he who is sent greater than he who sent him. If you know these things, blessed are you if you do them."

Quote For The Day
Elder Ephraim (Counsels from the Holy Mountain)
    Compel yourself, my child, for the sake of your soul. Compel yourself to comfort the brethren, and the Lord will comfort you, He will give you His grace. Have patience, have patience....Great is he who has more humility. God gives grace to the person who has fear of God and obeys everyone like a small child and

86

constantly seeks God's holy will. Such a person never seeks that his own will be done, but the will of God and of the others. ... So, my child, this is what you should do, too. This makes the demons tremble, flee far away, and not approach any more. They are very afraid when they see humility, obedience and love towards all. [26]

Reflect On This

You can imagine the perplexity of the disciples that evening in the upper room. Jesus took bread and wine and spoke of His body and blood, a reality that never fully sunk into their minds until after His death and resurrection. The evening was rich with symbolism, for after the supper was complete, Jesus' next action was something they weren't prepared for. Here was their Teacher and Lord assuming the role of a servant, kneeling before each of them to wash their feet. Bread and wine, towel and basin- these were symbols that would leave a life-long impression in their hearts and minds. The One whom they had come to know as Lord of all was here to be Servant of all in a service that would ultimately lead Him to the cross. For Jesus it wasn't merely words and symbols because His actions would bear out that He truly had a heart fitted for service, regardless of the cost.

In washing the feet of His disciples, Jesus was teaching them a lesson which would stand for all who desire to be His disciples. "For I have given you an example, that you also should do as I have done to you. Most assuredly, I say to you, a servant is not greater than his master, nor is he who is sent greater than he who sent him. If you know these things blessed are you if you do them."

Jesus was calling his disciples to a life of humble service, promising blessing, not in the knowing, but in the doing. As we are instructed in Philippians 2:5, "Let this mind be in you which was also in Christ Jesus," in the context of his humility and suffering as a servant who "made Himself of no reputation, taking the form of a bondservant." (Philippians 2:7). It begins in the mind, with a mindset of humility, service and putting others before yourself.

Too often the attitude is expressed by professing Christians today, "I don't get anything out of church. It just doesn't do anything for me." Have you ever felt that way, even if you haven't expressed it in words to anyone? Certainly the Orthodox Church is a place where we should receive instruction, fellowship, blessing and encouragement- all things we need. But it is *also* a place where we can serve others.

God gives you gifts and skills to be used for the benefit of others. People sometimes complain about not knowing their gifts or not knowing what they can do, when the deeper issue they need to face is, "Do I have a willingness and desire to serve others? Do I struggle with pride that would keep me from taking up the towel and basin?" Ministry to others, both within the Church and in the world, doesn't begin with an action plan. It begins with an attitude of the heart. Out of a heart fitted for service comes a plan of action that leads to ministry.

Humility is something difficult to grasp. That night in the upper room Peter struggled with it and his question, "Lord, are you going to wash my feet?" probably expressed what the others were thinking. Humility was a hard lesson for Peter to learn, and it usually is for us as well. Reflecting on the words of Jesus and the words from Elder Ephraim, we realize that what we are called to be and do is not easy. We cannot approach the challenge out of a heart of pride and self-will. Our hearts must be transformed by God's grace to be filled with humility and genuine love that is demonstrated in a servant attitude toward others.

Think, Respond And Apply
    1. Put yourself in the upper room that night with the disciples. You have seen Jesus work miracles. You have heard Him teaching. You accept that He is the Messiah, the Son of God.

How would you have reacted when He kneeled down to wash your feet? How does it make you feel now?

2. Have you ever gone through an experience with another person in need that has humbled you and caused you to see them as Jesus would? Has pride ever kept you from helping someone else, possibly because of their spiritual or social status, race or some other factor?

3. Do you actively look for opportunities for service in your local church and in your world, or do you wait for someone to point out a need or ask you to help?

4. Reflect on the words of today's quote. Relate those words to the attitude of your heart toward others. Spend some time in self-examination to determine if there are things in your life that are barriers to having a heart of humility that will free you to serve others. Talk to your priest and ask him about how you might be of more help to others in your church community.

Pray

Reflect on the words of Philippians 2:5-11 and the call to personal action called for in verse 5. Pray that God would place in your heart a desire for that mind like Christ. Ask God to convict you and bring to your attention issues of pride and resistance that would hinder you from serving others.

WEEK FOUR
DAY TWENTY-THREE

UNDERSTANDING MY RESPONSIBILITY

Scriptures For The Day
Ephesians 4:14-16
...That we should no longer be children, tossed to and fro and carried about by every wind of doctrine, by the trickery of men, in the cunning craftiness of deceitful plotting, but, speaking the truth in love, may grow up in all things into Him, who is the head- Christ- from whom the whole body, joined and knit together by what every joint supplies, according to the effective working by which every part does its share, causes growth of the body for the edifying of itself in love.
Proverbs 3:27
Do not withhold good from those to whom it is due, when it is in the power of your hand to do so.

Quote For The Day
Elder Ephriam (Counsels from the Holy Mountain)
Great is our honor- though unworthy- to have been called by God to serve in the work of saving souls as His tools, bearing in mind that if others (apostles, etc) had not sacrificed their lives for our sake, we would not be children of God and heirs of heavenly blessings. Therefore let us do whatever we can; the work will be completed by Him Who has the power to perfect it. Think about how the first Christians struggled during the times of the catacombs; with what self-sacrifice, with what love they sacrificed things dear to them when Christian duty called. And in the end, their sacrifices brought them eternal glory.[27]

Reflect On This

There is a concept existing within the thousands of "denominations" in the Protestant churches which says all I have to do is believe in Jesus and I will go to heaven. It's as simple as that: "just believe!"

Such "easy believism" has no relationship with the call of Jesus to a life of committed, active discipleship. James said that the demons believe and shudder (James 2:19). But what good does that do them? You enter the doorway to salvation through your conversion, through your baptism, but that entrance takes you into a new life with new responsibilities. We are told in Romans 6:4, "Therefore we were buried with him through baptism into death, that just as Christ was raised from the dead by the glory of the Father, even so we also should walk in newness of life." We are told in verse 22 of that chapter that we have been freed from the slavery to sin and "having become slaves of God" in order to live a life of obedience to God. We enter into a new life in Christ with a responsibility to live in newness of life, and we enter into a new relationship, no longer enslaved to sin, but now enslaved to God and responsible to live as belonging to God.

Today's Scriptures point out our personal responsibility. Ephesians four portrays the Church as a body and every member a vital part of the body. Using this analogy the Apostle Paul stresses our personal responsibility: we "may grow up in all things into Him who is the head, Christ." Just as our physical bodies grow as each individual part grows together toward physical maturity, so in the Orthodox Church each member is responsible to grow toward spiritual maturity. What does that involve for you? It certainly means much more than filling your mind with the theology of the faith, not to discredit theology. It implies the ongoing transformation of your life, which will be evidenced by your ministry within the Church: "as each part is working properly, promotes the body's growth in building itself up in love." The "every part does its share" includes you. The healthy life of the

Church is not only dependent on its bishops and priests but also on every member. This reality is stressed throughout the New Testament epistles.

Your responsibility in the Church relates to its inner function and growth as well as its outward mission in the world. Wherever the Church finds itself, the need is there to proclaim the gospel and reach out in the love of Christ to a world in need. It means working together for peace, justice and alleviating the pain and suffering of so many in our world in the name of Jesus. Proverbs 3:27 has application to a multitude of situations and needs in our world today and would be a good proverb to commit to memory- "Do not withhold good from those to whom it is due, when it is in the power of your hand to do so." God gives you gifts, skills, material and financial resources to use in ministering to others in the Church and in your world.

Don't become too comfortable in what you know and assume someone else will do what needs to be done. As the old saying goes, you have to walk your talk. Take your God-given responsibilities seriously and make a difference in your local church and in your world.

Think, Respond And Apply

1. This may take some time and thought, but it will be personally beneficial. Focus first on your local church. What are your responsibilities to your church and in what ways can you fulfill them? Write them down and be specific in terms of fulfillment. Next, focus on your world, beginning with your community around you. What are your responsibilities to your world and in what ways can you fulfill them? In both of these areas take into consideration your God-given gifts and skills as well as your material and financial resources. This exercise can help you formulate a personal vision statement and a game plan for practically fulfilling your responsibilities as a Christian.

2. Have you ever been in a situation where you have had the opportunity to do good to someone but failed to do anything? How did it make you feel? Did you regret your inaction later? Did you learn from your experience?

Pray

You have the great privilege of being a recipient of the love and mercy of God, as well as being a member of the Body of Christ, the Church. Express your thankfulness to God for this. Ask God to enable you to become more aware of your responsibilities and to have the wisdom to know how to best fulfill them.

WEEK FOUR
DAY TWENTY-FOUR

WORSHIP: A FORETASTE OF HEAVEN

Scripture For The Day
Revelation 5:11-14
Then I looked, and I heard the voice of many angels around the throne, the living creatures and the elders; and the number of them was ten thousand times ten thousand and thousands of thousands, saying with a loud voice: "Worthy is the Lamb that was slain to receive power and riches and wisdom, and strength and honor and glory and blessing!" And every creature which is in heaven and on earth and under the earth and such as are in the sea, and all that are in them, I heard saying: "Blessing and honor and glory and power be to Him who sits on the throne, and to the Lamb, forever and ever." Then the four living creatures said, "Amen!" And the twenty-four elders fell down and worshiped Him who lives forever and ever.

Quote For The Day
Bishop Kallistos Ware (The Orthodox Church)
    The Holy Liturgy is something that embraces two worlds at once, for both in heaven and on earth the Liturgy is one and the same- one altar, one sacrifice, one presence. In every place of worship, however humble its outward appearance, as the faithful gather to perform the Eucharist, they are taken up into the 'heavenly places'; in every place of worship when the Holy Sacrifice is offered, not merely the local congregation is present, but the Church universal- the saints, the angels, the Mother of God, and Christ Himself. 'Now the celestial powers are present with us, and worship invisibly' (words sung at the Great Entrance in the Liturgy of the Presanctified). This we know, that God dwells there among humans. Orthodox, inspired by this vision of heaven on

earth, have striven to make their worship in outward splendor and beauty an icon of the Great Liturgy in heaven. [28]

Reflect On This

Do you live from one week to the next looking forward to the high point of your week in the worship service of your church? Does a sense of awe and reverence fill your heart as you come before the Lord in worship with the Church? Or do you dread it a bit and find yourself struggling to stay awake for the hour? So what does worship have to do with ministry anyway?

When we come before God in worship as the Church together we are engaged in the highest form of ministry, our ministry to God. There is nothing that delights the heart of God more than the praise and worship of the Church and today's Scripture shows it in its highest expression in the very heavenly presence of God. In fact, our corporate worship from week to week is to be a small taste of heaven where we will worship God, Father, Son and Holy Spirit, in the fullness of divine splendor.

Our worship is an offering to God that goes far beyond what we put in the collection plate each week. The important question isn't, "What do I get out of worship?", but rather, "What do I go prepared to give in worship?" You see, what you gain from worship by way of blessing, instruction, comfort and help is secondary. These are byproducts of worship. *The primary issue is what you are giving to God each week in worship.*

How prepared are you to enter the church sanctuary on Sunday morning to present an offering to God? The preparation must take place before you ever get to the church door, through your personal worship and devotion during the week. That will take effort and personal preparation on your part, and through your regular participation in the sacrament of confession with your priest or spiritual father.

The common attitude today for people going to a worship service is to view it like a concert or theatrical performance in which they are no more than spectators watching what unfolds before them. When the performance is good enough they may even applaud. No wonder many church goers today hunger for an authentic worship experience. The worship liturgy in the Orthodox Church is designed to draw every person present into active participation.

Another characteristic of our day is an uncertainty on the part of many non-Orthodox Christians as to what worship is to be, which results in just about anything passing for worship. Yet we see in Scripture and in the tradition of the Church from its beginning that worship has a clear focus and definite components.

The focus of worship must be on God. To focus on anything else is not worship. There is a danger today in the modern Protestant "seeker sensitive" emphasis to put more focus on the comfort and relaxed atmosphere of the congregation than on the glory of God. Who says worship should make us feel comfortable? Realizing that we are entering the presence of the Lord God Almighty, our worship should leave us with a sense of awe and humility. Our primary concern should be making God feel at home in the worship we are offering.

When you begin to look at worship from the context of Scripture and history you discover some important components that work together to glorify God. Worship should involve praise, proclamation, intercession and sacrament. We lift up our hearts and voices in praise to God. We invoke God's presence in our midst and acknowledge our need of and dependence on a God of mercy and compassion who hears our confession, our intercession and all of our corporate prayers. We listen to God's written word read and proclaimed and respond in our hearts to its message, hopefully in a way that will impact our living before God. We offer to God bread and wine and in return partake of the Body and Blood of Christ and give thanks for so great a gift and so great a salvation. In worship we offer ourselves to God and through all of our senses and out of the abundance of our hearts we interact with God who is in our midst.

Worship is not a passive experience, let alone entertainment, or even education. It demands your preparation, your involvement, your ministry to God who is there to meet with you each week.

Think, Respond And Apply

1. Reflect on today's quote. Does it introduce you to a new and deeper concept of what the weekly worship experience of the Church is? How does it expand your understanding of worship? Does it raise any questions in relation to worship?

2. In your Sunday worship experience do you see yourself as a spectator or a participant? If you say spectator, how do you view what is happening on Sunday morning? If you say participant what does that involve for you?

3. On Sunday morning as you go to church how prepared are you to worship? What do you consider to be important in your preparation?

4. When you consider the awesome vision of worship in today's Scripture, what connection do you see in your Sunday worship with this great event? Does your worship ever cause you to wonder what heaven will be like?

Pray

Pray that God would enlarge your vision of worship to understand its true significance before God and its importance as a ministry of all God's people. Pray for a greater capacity for personal involvement in worship each week.

PRAY FOR ONE ANOTHER

Scripture For The Day
Ephesians 6:18-2
...Praying always with all prayer and supplication in the Spirit,
being watchful to this end with all perseverance and supplication
for all the saints- and for me, that utterance may be given to me,
that I may open my mouth boldly to make known the mystery of
the gospel, for which I am an ambassador in chains, that in it I may
speak boldly, as I ought to speak.

Quote For The Day
St. John Chrysostom (On Prayer)
   But it is laid on you, to make intercession for the whole world,
for the Church spread to the ends of the earth, and for those who
minister in it, and preside over it... How much greater a task is it,
do you think, for our littleness to go to God, and beseech Him for
so many people? For if I have not confidence enough to intercede
for myself, much less have I got it for others; this is a task for those
who are worthy... For if the prayer of the Church helped Peter,
and delivered that Pillar from the prison, how can you, I ask you,
ignore its power? For as the power of love is not broken by
distance, neither is the efficacy of prayer... And you say: What
need have I of prayers? You need them for this reason: because
you think that you have no need of them. [29]

Reflect On This
   "If I can't do anything else for you, at least I can always pray
for you." Have you ever had anyone say this to you, or have you
ever told anyone this? Words like these reflect the attitude that
prayer is a last resort. When all else is done and there are no more

options, then you can always pray. Does this seem to express an exaggeration or reality? It would appear today in many churches where corporate prayer plays a very minor role, if any at all, that this is the true picture. In many Protestant churches today the prayer meeting is an event of the past, or if it still continues is often just kept alive by a handful of older members who still see value in it.

Today's quote begins with this statement, "But it is laid on you, to make intercession for the whole world, for the Church spread to the ends of the earth." Now that's a huge demand placed on each believer. Does the New Testament support this statement in the place it gives prayer ministry in the Church? What role does prayer play in the life of the Church in the Book of Acts and in the epistles? Think of the Church's prayers for Peter, mentioned by St. John Chrysostom in today's quote.

We discover in Acts that in the beginning as the disciples waited for the promised Holy Spirit they were focused on one thing: "These all continued with one accord with prayer and supplication, with the women and Mary the mother of Jesus, and with His brothers." (Acts 1:14). Throughout the Book of Acts prayer was woven into the fabric of the life of the early church. The emphasis becomes even stronger in the epistles, especially those of the Apostle Paul, who continually emphasized the ministry of prayer and often prayed for those to whom he wrote.

Today's Scripture puts prayer in the context of an exhortation on spiritual warfare in which the Apostle Paul challenges Christians to put on the whole armor of God for their spiritual battles. Prayer is seen as an important force in those spiritual battles, not just prayer for ourselves, but prayer for one another, prayer as a vital ministry. "...praying always with all prayer and supplication in the Spirit, being watchful to this end with all perseverance and supplication for all the saints." Notice the emphasis in the words used- "always, being watchful, always with all perseverance." The Apostle sees prayer as a vital ministry for the Church, not a last resort when all else has been tried, but a front line spiritual ministry.

In some ways we have convinced ourselves that we have advanced beyond the place of needing prayer as much as the Church did in the past. Prayer to a certain degree has become obsolete. When we need to get something done we can always employ the latest guaranteed program, or bring in the big name profession in an up-to-date video conference, or set up a study group to solve problems. Of course with any of these we should at least ask God to bless our efforts, so that would involve prayer. Now that may sound somewhat cynical, but in reality it portrays what has happened to prayer in many churches today. Why pray when we can be doing something more practical that will be achieving "results" now?

You don't need any special gifts or a seminary degree to pray. You simply need a compassion for people in their needs and a faith in God before whom you bring your prayers. As today's quote says, "For if the prayer of the Church helped Peter, and delivered that Pillar from the prison, how can you, I ask you, ignore its power? For if the power of love is not broken by distance, neither is the efficacy of prayer."

What do you believe God can do? Maybe you don't believe God is quite as capable as the latest program or fad that seems to be catching on like wild fire. Do you believe that prayer would really make a difference in the Church and in all it attempts to do for God?

When it comes to ministry in the Church today, there is none more important than prayer. The Church needs to recapture this vision. You can be a vital part of this ministry in your local church community.

Think, Respond And Apply

1. What role does prayer play in the life of your local church? Is it seen as priority ministry? Where would it fit on a scale of 1-10, with 10 being most important? Why?

2. How actively involved are you in praying for people in your church, for your bishops and priests, people with special needs and the Church's missions?

3. Can you see yourself as a catalyst for change in bringing prayer to a greater place of prominence in your church? What could you do personally to promote the ministry of prayer?

4. Consider beginning a prayer journal. Keep a record of needs, individuals, ministries that need your prayers. If your local church has a photo directory of its members this could be used as a guide. Be organized and see this as an important ministry you can have to your church.

Pray

Focus your prayers today on your church. Pray for the leaders and the membership in general, the ministries it's involved in and the needs you know of. Pray that God would help you and others with your church to capture a vision of the important role of prayer ministry.

WEEK FOUR
DAY TWENTY-SIX

A HEART FOR MY WORLD

Scripture For The Day
Matthew 9:35-38
Then Jesus went about all the cities and villages, teaching in their
synagogues, preaching the gospel of the kingdom, and healing
every sickness and every disease among the people. But when he
saw the multitudes, He was moved with compassion for them,
because they were weary and scattered, like sheep having no
shepherd. Then He said to his disciples, "The harvest truly is
plentiful, but the laborers are few. Therefore pray the Lord of the
harvest to send out laborers into His harvest."

Quote For The Day
Jordan Bajis (Common Ground)
      Catholicity [in other words the universality of the Orthodox
Church] has been given to the Church; but its achievement is the
Church's task. We have a necessary part to play... Each is called
to reveal Christ's wholeness, love and redemption within the
Church, and then to bring that catholicity into the world by loving
as Christ loves. This inner 'catholic consciousness' of the Church
will only be revealed when her members take steps of faith, and
when they open their lives to one another in heart and mind. Such
an active catholic community will have no 'barriers', whether they
be national, regional, racial, sexual, economic, cultural or social.
All these divisions will be overcome by God's love. 30

Reflect On This
      "When He saw the multitudes He was moved with
compassion for them, because they were weary and scattered, like
sheep having no shepherd." These words reveal to us the heart of

Jesus as He walked this earth. Wherever He went during His public ministry the crowds followed Him. Many were just curious, wondering what He was going to say or do next. But many were there in desperation and need. Jesus reached out to heal the blind, the lame, the deaf, the lepers, and even to raise the dead. Yet it is very evident that the compassion of Jesus went beyond the physical needs of people. He was able to see into the hearts of hurting people, people enslaved by sins, in bondage to pride, greed, lust, whatever the sin was, weighed down by guilt, and in desperate need of forgiveness and restoration. He came to set the captive free. This was His mission, as set forth in the Scripture He read in the synagogue at the beginning of His earthly ministry (Luke 4:16-21). He came to "proclaim liberty to the captives and recovery of sight to the blind, to set at liberty those who are oppressed, to proclaim the acceptable year of the Lord." His ministry gave evidence to this mandate, which was fulfilled, not out of mere duty but out of a heart of compassion for the world.

Do you prefer the comfort and security of a tightly knit group of Christians or are you challenged by the needs and opportunities in your world today? In Jesus' ministry to His disciples there was a balance between teaching, nurturing and equipping them and sending them out into the world after the manner of ministry He had patterned for them. After his resurrection he challenged them with the mandate of Acts 1:8 and following the Day of Pentecost the Church began to move out from Jerusalem, to Judea, to Samaria, and then to the ends of the earth. It was a church with a heart for its world, regardless of the reaction the world had toward it. Ultimately for many they would pay the price of their lives to love the world as Jesus did.

Today's quote points us to the heart of Christian discipleship: "Each is called to reveal Christ's wholeness, love and redemption within the Church, and then to bring that catholicity into the world by loving as Christ loves." It is interesting that compassion for our world is tied to the catholic (or universal) nature of the Orthodox

Church, which can only be fulfilled in a practical way by Christians truly revealing Christ's "wholeness, love and redemption within the Church."

Developing a heart for my world is an overflow from the true nature of my heart for the Orthodox Church. How we live together within the context of the Church will reveal how we will relate to our world outside and how we respond to the reality of "For God so loved the world He gave His only begotten Son…" (John 3:16). This is a world in rebellion, estranged by sin, yet God loves it to the extent of sending Jesus Christ. Why would God bother? Why? Because that demonstrates who our God is and what love is, from the humble birth in a manger to the agonizing death on a cross, under the indescribable weight of human sin. It's from this background that we come to understand in some small way the compassion Jesus had for the people He ministered to. It was a costly, sacrificial giving out of a heart of love for the world.

If you are going to live as a disciple of Jesus you must be willing to follow in His footsteps. That means you must come to see your world through the eyes of Jesus, to see people in their need as Jesus saw them and be moved with compassion toward them. You must be willing to love as Jesus loves and give yourself, even sacrificially if need be, to minister to people. Multitudes live in spiritual darkness, needing the light of the gospel of Jesus Christ. Multitudes live in poverty, abuse, suffering, injustice. What will you do for them? How will you respond to their cries for help?

There is no place to stand aloof, to be wrapped up in your own comfortable Christian world, insulated from the pain of others. "Such an active catholic community will have no 'barriers', whether they be national, regional, racial, sexual, economic, cultural or social. All these divisions will be overcome by God's love." Living out this degree of catholic unity within the Church will allow us to move without barriers into our world with Christ's love and compassion. Let your heart be broken with those things that break the heart of God. Don't buy into the narcissistic attitudes of our culture, but let God mold your heart to truly be a heart for your world.

Think, Respond And Apply

1. How much time do you spend with and how do you interact with non-Christian people? What opportunities do you use to reach out to others in practical ways?

2. Look seriously at your neighborhood, your town or city. What do you see as needs that Christians should be involved in? What do you see that you could do? Is there anything in particular that burdens your heart?

3. God's love, we are told in today's quote, is self-giving love, free of barriers, and that truth is so evident throughout Scripture. Do you have any personal fears or concerns when you think about your need to have a heart with the compassion of Jesus for your world?

4. How outwardly-focused is your local church? What active involvement does it have in its community, in ministering where the needs are? Can you be a catalyst to stir your Orthodox community to more active involvement if the need is there?

Pray

When Jesus prayed in the garden, "O My Father, if it is possible, let this cup pass from Me; nevertheless, not as I will but as You will." (Matthew 26:39), He was struggling with the great personal price of God's self-giving love. He alone, as our Savior, could pay that price. But there is a price to be paid in having a heart for your world. Pray that God would open your eyes to see your world in all its need, as God sees it. Pray that God would burden your heart in a way that would lead you to live out your love for your world in some way each day.

WEEK FOUR
DAY TWENTY-SEVEN

DOING JUSTICE IN JESUS' NAME

Scriptures For The Day
Isaiah 58:6-9
Is this not the fast that I have chosen: to lose the bonds of
wickedness, to undo the heavy burdens, to let the oppressed go
free, and that you break every yoke? Is it not to share your bread
with the hungry, and that you bring to your house the poor that are
cast out; when you see the naked, that you cover him, and not hide
yourself from your own flesh? Then your light shall break forth
like the morning, your healing shall spring forth speedily, and your
righteousness shall go before you; the glory of the Lord shall be
your rear guard. Then you shall call, and the Lord will answer; you
shall cry, and He will say, "Here I am."
Luke 4:16-21
So He came to Nazareth, where He had been brought up. And as
His custom was, He went into the synagogue on the Sabbath day,
and stood up to read. And He was handed the book of the prophet
Isaiah. And when He had opened the book, He found the place
where it was written: "The Spirit of the Lord is upon Me, because
He has anointed Me to preach the gospel to the poor; He has sent
Me to heal the brokenhearted, to proclaim liberty to the captives
and recovery of sight to the blind, to set at liberty those who are
oppressed; to proclaim the acceptable year of the Lord." Then He
closed the book, and gave it back to the attendant and sat down.
And the eyes of all who were in the synagogue were fixed on Him.
And He began to say to them, "Today this Scripture is fulfilled in
your hearing."

Quote For The Day
Mother Maria of Paris
    The bodies of our fellow human beings must be treated with more care than our own. Christian love teaches us to give our brethren not only spiritual gifts, but material gifts as well. Even our last shirt, our last piece of bread must be given to them. Personal almsgiving and the most wide-ranging social work are equally justifiable and necessary.
    The way to God lies through love of other people, and there is no other way. At the Last Judgment I shall not be asked if I was successful in my ascetic exercises or how many prostrations I made in the course of my prayers. I shall be asked, did I feed the hungry, clothe the naked, visit the sick and the prisoners: that is all I shall be asked.[31]

Reflect On This
    The issue of justice is a biblical issue, not just for the prophets of the Old Testament, but for all of God's people in all times. Because we are in the world as salt and light, our presence is to permeate the darkness of sin and injustice and in the name of Jesus we are to speak for and defend those whose voice is not heard. We must understand in a practical way that to know God is to do justice.
    Maybe your reaction is, "The church is here to save souls. Its business is spiritual. What does God have to do with issues of justice anyway?" Sometimes we may fail to realize that God created us as whole people, not disembodied souls, and redemption and re-creation involves the whole person. God also created us as relational and social beings and the original purpose in creation was for those relationships and that society to glorify God. Our willful rebellion and disobedience has not only affected our relationship with God, but also our relationship with each other. Christians are called to be agents of reconciliation (2 Corinthians

5:17-20), calling people to a right relationship with God and hand-in-hand with that, to a right relationship with each other.

The prophet Isaiah, in today's Scripture, speaks for God in calling people not only to observe the spiritual discipline of fasting, but out of their fasting to go further beyond themselves and fight for justice on behalf of the oppressed, the hungry, the homeless, the poor, those who are held in "the bonds of wickedness." The prophetic call resonates throughout the Old Testament and is refocused by Jesus on His own ministry, as defined in Luke 4:18,19. Jesus came "to preach the gospel to the poor, proclaim liberty to the captives and recovery of sight to the blind, to set at liberty those who are oppressed, to proclaim the acceptable year of the Lord." It is evident by Jesus' ministry that there is a twofold application to the fulfillment of this statement. He met the deepest need of reconciliation with God in those He ministered to, yet at the same time transformed the situations many found themselves in.

Christians living in the affluent West have a greater responsibility in matters of justice in our world, whether it is matters of racial tensions, poverty, homelessness or the many issues of discrimination present in our society or political repression, starvation and poverty, ethnic injustice or a lack of respect for the sanctity of the lives of the unborn, elderly and handicapped, and many other issues around our world.

What a great need there is for the clear voice of Christians to speak out, the finances of Christians to help, and the presence of Christians who are willing to take risks for the benefit of others in great need. It isn't enough to say, "God cares and understands your pain." As Proverbs 3:27 instructs us, "Do not withhold good from those to whom it is due, when it is in the power of your hand to do so." What a challenge that is for each of us.

What can you do? Begin by asking God to give you a greater sensitivity to issues of justice in your neighborhood and around the world. Open your eyes to see. Read, listen and be informed. There are Christian organizations working in the forefront of justice issues around the world. Outside of the Church there are larger and broader-based organizations that are standing up and acting on behalf of oppressed and suffering people and making the world aware of issues of injustice globally. Most have web sites where you can find out more information. Be willing to write to political leaders on behalf of victims of injustice. When issues are close to home write letters to editors of newspapers and see where you can be involved as a volunteer. In our information age saying, "I didn't know," is no longer a valid excuse because it is so easy to become well informed.

The early Christians lived by the standard of the love of Jesus in a way that baffled outsiders. They loved friend and foe alike and were there to minister in Jesus' name. They stood firm against the abuses and injustices of Rome and suffered for it. They cared for those who were mistreated and abandoned by society. They willingly helped the helpless and protected the widows, orphans, the unborn babies, the handicapped and outcasts. No, the Church hasn't always been a champion of justice and for that it bears guilt, but if it stands true to its calling in Christ, it will be there with the love of Christ in the midst of pain, suffering and injustice.

Think, Respond And Apply

1. Can you think of an issue in your community/city that is an issue relating to justice? On a national level, can you think of three present day issues that relate to justice? On a global scale, can you think of three present day issues that relate to justice?

2. How does God demonstrate concern for justice in the Old Testament? Can you think of any specific examples? How did Jesus in the New Testament demonstrate a concern for justice in the light of his reading of the prophetic word in Luke 4:16-21?

3. Are there justice issues in your world today that weigh heavily on your heart? What could you do to demonstrate your Christian love and responsibility in relation to the issue(s)?

4. Over the next week as you read the newspaper and watch or listen to the news, look for news items, editorials, etc., that relate to justice issues and about which Christians should have an active concern. Make a list of those things you come across during the week.

Pray

Acknowledging that justice is a matter close to the heart of God, pray that God would help you to be more aware of injustice on every level in your world. Pray for wisdom to know how to respond and to know what you can do to make a difference.

WEEK FOUR
DAY TWENTY-EIGHT

REMEMBER, THE CHURCH BELONGS TO GOD

Scriptures For The Day
Ephesians 1:22,23
And He put all things under His feet, and gave Him to be head over all things to the church, which is His body, the fullness of Him who fills all in all.
Ephesians 2:19-22
Now, therefore, you are no longer strangers and foreigners, but fellow citizens with the saints and members of the household of God, having been built on the foundation of the apostles and prophets, Jesus Christ Himself being the chief cornerstone, in whom the whole building, being fitted together, grows into a holy temple in the Lord, in whom you also are being built together for a dwelling place of God in the Spirit.

Quote For The Day
Jordan Bajis (Common Ground)
   The Church can never be separated from Christ…The book of Ephesians says this very thing when it refers to the Church as "His body, the fullness of Him who fills all in all" (Eph.1:23). The Word "fullness" here is the Greek word pleroma which means "that which makes something full or complete." In this light, the Ephesian passage reveals an amazing and incomprehensible mystery: we, as the Church, somehow actually supplement, and complement, Christ Himself! How can this be? In Christ, the Church stands as a new humanity (1 Cor. 15:20-23), redeemed and reborn through her Head. The depth and intensity of our intimacy with Christ unfolds the mystery of His existence within the Church." [32]

111

Reflect On This

We are called to use our gifts for the good of the body of Christ, the Church (Romans 12:3-8). We exercise our ministry in and through the church. The New Testament has nothing to say about professing Christians living apart from the Church and serving God. Only the narcissistic individualism of today would consider that to be acceptable. While functioning within the Orthodox Church as a member of the body, contributing to the growth and health of the body, we always need to remember whose body it is.

Scripture gives us word pictures to present truth in an understandable way. St. Paul presents the Church as the body of Christ, "His body, the fullness of Him who fills all in all." It is Christ's Church, not ours. We may be part of it, but we don't own it. There is a need for Christians today to reacquaint themselves with this perspective, for it seems at times that many have forgotten who the Church belongs to.

Some would handle the Church as their own personal possession with the attitude that they have the freedom to make the Church anything they want it to be. Some regard the Church as their own personal servant, there to meet their every whim and desire, and if it fails they will shop around for another one. So many prevalent attitudes and actions among professing Christians would cause one to wonder if they really know who the Church belongs to.

The Ephesian epistle focuses strongly on the Church, how and why it exists. Today's quote is rooted in an Ephesian perspective. Today's Scripture challenges believers to look up and see their high and holy calling in Christ, as well as to see the high and holy reality of the Church. You are "fellow citizens with the saints, members of the household of God... built together for a dwelling place of God." Here we get a glimpse of the spiritual and mystical nature of the Orthodox Church, and the Church we see portrayed isn't a human creation but a divine one. It's a temple where God

112

dwells. This is nothing ordinary and commonplace. Sometimes we lose sight of this truth because the Church is made up of ordinary people with all their faults and idiosyncrasies. There are no perfect local churches and no perfect Christians, but we are all in the process of becoming what God desires us to be in Christ. The local churches are always "under construction," always becoming, never arriving, until that day when it stands transformed in the presence of its head, Jesus Christ.

In 1 Corinthians 3:16,17 the warning was given to the Corinthian Christians to realize who the Church belonged to and how it is to be treated: "Do you not know that you are the temple of God and that the Spirit of dwells in you? If anyone defiles the temple of God, God will destroy him. For the temple of God is holy, which temple you are."

God has called you to live, to grow, to exercise your gifts and ministry as part of the Church. What a great privilege this is. What a great opportunity you have. Just keep in the forefront of your mind whose Body it is and that reality will govern your attitudes and actions.

Think, Respond And Apply

1. Do you find it hard to grasp the reality of today's focus that the Orthodox Church belongs to God and not to us? What are some barriers you may face in relation to this?

2. Reflect on the words of today's quote. Think about the sense of "amazing and incomprehensible mystery" in relation to the Church, as the body of Christ, as Bajis says, we "somehow actually supplement, and complement Christ Himself." Think on this and write down your thoughts about it.

3. Does the fact of God's ownership of the Church cause you to see your ministry and the exercise of your gifts differently? Does this truth impact your attitude toward what you do in the Church?

4. Do you find it easy to be negative and critical about the Church? As today's Scripture says, as a member you are a citizen with the saints and a member of God's household. In light of this reality, think of definite ways you can become a catalyst for positive change in your church and through your personal ministries work to build it up.

Pray

Pray that God would enlarge your vision to see the Church from the perspective of today's Scripture. If you struggle at times with a negative and critical attitude toward the Church and the people in it, ask God to give you a heart for the Church and its members that would be positive and glorifying to Christ.

POSTSCRIPT 1
DAY THIRTY

MOVING CLOSER TO THE GOAL

Scriptures For The Day
Hebrews 12:1,2
Therefore we also, since we are surrounded by so great a cloud of witnesses, let us lay aside every weight, and the sin which so easily ensnares us, and let us run with endurance the race that is set before us, looking unto Jesus, the author and finisher of our faith, who for the joy that was set before Him endured the cross, despising the shame, and has sat down at the right hand of the throne of God.
Philippians 3:13,14
Brethern, I do not count myself to have apprehended; but one thing I do, forgetting those things which are behind and reaching forward to those things which are ahead, I press toward the goal for the prize of the upward call of God in Christ Jesus.

Quote For The Day
Niketas Stethatos
Once a soul has been consumed in the depths of God's love and has tasted the sweet delight of God's intellective graces, it can no longer bear to stay frozen in its former condition but is impelled to rise ever higher to the heavens. The higher it ascends through the Spirit, and the deeper it sinks into the abyss of God, the more it is consumed by the fire of longing and searches out the immensity of the even deeper mysteries of God, strenuously trying to come into that blessed light, where every intellect is caught up into ecstasy, where the heart knows it can finally rest from all its strivings and find its rest in joy. [34]

Reflect On This

There is a vast difference between a marathon runner and a short distance sprinter, although both demand training and discipline. The sprinter explodes from the blocks to expend a maximum amount of energy in a matter of seconds. The marathon runner has a whole different perspective, conserving energy for the long haul. There has to be a steady focus toward the goal with the understanding that it is not a momentary achievement. There must be stamina and physical reserves to carry the marathon runner through to the end of the race, while at the starting line the end may seem like a hundred miles away to an amateur.

The Christian life is much like a marathon and in fact is portrayed that way in Hebrews 12:1,2 and in Philippians 3:13,14. It's interesting how the race motif is used in the New Testament to portray the Christian life. You have come a long way in this present project of spiritual makeover and if you have faithfully moved from one day to the next you may feel somewhat like a marathon runner as you close in on day thirty. But this is just one month out of your life, even if it proves to be a very transformational month. What you have learned, experienced and applied to your life needs to be followed through for the rest of your life- that's the whole race.

Sometimes we find ourselves so caught up in the daily routine that we lose sight of the bigger picture and fail to set our goals in the light of the greater marathon we are in, instead of just the daily sprints. Now the daily sprints can be challenging- facing career, family obligations, social and financial expectations, and any number of unexpected interruptions- and all this demands daily focus and discipline. But those days are part of weeks, months and years, the whole panorama of your life. That's the bigger picture, the marathon.

Over this month you have been building spiritual resources for the daily sprints, as well as for the longer marathon of your life. You have tasted of the disciplines, challenges and resources that

116

are at your disposal. Hopefully you have come to know God a bit better, discovered some new things about yourself, and have tested some of the spiritual tools that equip you for the life of discipleship.

How have you responded to the greatness of the possibilities that are before you as well as the limitless potential of your life before God? What a challenge that is! Has your heart been stirred and challenged? Today's quote challenges you further, "Once a soul has been consumed in the depths of God's love and has tasted the sweet delight of God's intellective graces, it can no longer stay frozen in its own former condition but is impelled to rise even higher to the heavens." That's the image conveyed in Philippians 3:13,14, "forgetting those things which are behind and reaching forward to what those things which are ahead."

You can close your eyes and picture the image of the runner in the race. There is no looking back, no slowing down; every ounce of energy is poured into crossing the finish line. Hebrews 12:1,2 paints the same picture, but it adds one important perspective. There at the finish line is seated the one who has run the race for us and who, through his victory, enables us to endure and ultimately achieve the goal: "looking unto Jesus the author and finisher of our faith, who for the joy that was set before Him endured the cross, despising the shame, and has sat down at the right hand of the throne of God."

You are "the joy that was set before him"- all those He died to redeem, and he is the goal we are moving toward. Focus your eyes on Jesus as you move closer to the goal and know with assurance that through Him you can make it.

Think, Respond And Apply

1. Do you find yourself at times getting bogged down in the details of daily living and losing sight of the bigger picture? That's one of the hazards of life we all face. Reflect on how making the

117

spiritual disciplines you have focused on this month part of your daily life, will help you to keep the bigger picture in focus.

2. Hebrews 12:1,2 speaks of running light, taking off the weights and "the sin which so easily ensnares us." As you examine your life what can you see as weights and sins that hinder you from becoming the person God desires you to be? How will you deal with these things in your life?

3. Today's quote speaks of coming to the place "where the heart knows it can finally rest from all its strivings and find its rest in joy." How does the prospect of moving toward that place in your life affect you? What desire does it create in your heart?

4. Being focused is a key to achieving goals. Life can be so easily fragmented by the demands, expectations and pressures you face daily. Consider the time you spend with God daily, as well as your worship on Sunday, as opportunities to bring all the daily details into the light of the bigger picture. In your daily journal bring together these two perspectives and reflect on them for your life.

Pray

Jesus Christ has run the race and finished the course for you. In Him you have found mercy, forgiveness, peace, love and hope. Pray that God would enable you to keep focused in your daily life and not lose sight of the ultimate goal. Sometimes like Peter stepping out of the boat to walk on the water to Jesus but sinking when he looks at the waves, we do the same thing. God's purpose for you is to reach the goal in Christ. This month has awakened you in a greater way to the reality of the goal. Pray that God would enable you to set aside the weights, deal with the sins that so easily ensnare, and run free toward Christ.

POSTSCRIPT 2
DAY THIRTY-ONE

WITHIN YOUR GRASP

Scripture For The Day
2 Peter 1:3,4
His divine power has given us all things that pertain to life and godliness, through the knowledge of Him who called us by glory and virtue, by which have been given to us exceeding great and precious promises, that through these you may be partakers of the divine nature, having escaped the corruption that is in the world through lust.

Quote For The Day
St. Makarios the Great
Even worldly persons desire to be associated with the glory of an earthly king. How much more true is this of those whom the finger of the divine Spirit of Life has touched. Divine love has wounded their hearts with the longing for Christ, the true and heavenly King. His beauty and ineffable glory, His unfailing graciousness, and His incomprehensible majesty have conspired to hold them captive with desire and longing. Their whole being is fixed upon Him. 34

Reflect On This
As you began this one month spiritual journey you entered it with a realization of personal needs as well as expectations. It's apparent that you have followed through to completion, but in reality this isn't the end, but just the beginning. Why did you begin in the first place? Were you struggling with frustration or disappointment in your spiritual life? Were you looking for a spiritual roadmap to help you along your personal pilgrimage?

Now that you have arrived at this point where do you want to go from here?

Have you ever found yourself so immersed in a good novel that you wanted it to never end? Have you ever tried a new food and discovered it to be so delicious that it had to become a regular part of your diet? It's interesting how things can capture us as they do and increase our desire for them. On a far grander scale is the hunger of our soul for God once we have tasted the riches of grace and mercy in Christ. This reality is brought out in today's quote, in speaking of Jesus Christ, "His beauty and ineffable glory, His unfailing graciousness, and His incomprehensible majesty have conspired to hold them captive with desire and longing. Their whole being is fixed upon him."

This is what God desires for each of us, that our whole being would be captivated with Jesus Christ and in Him our souls would be satisfied. But is this an elusive dream, a never-ending quest that results in ongoing frustration? At times in our human experience it may appear to be that way, but not by God's design or purpose.

The words of today's Scripture give hope and reassurance in your spiritual quest. "His divine power has given us all things that pertain to life and godliness, through the knowledge of Him who called us by glory and virtue."

Stop! Read that statement again and let it sink in for a moment. God's power- and that is without limit- is the source from which we receive everything- that's what it says, everything- needed for life and godliness. Everything! And it all comes through our knowledge of God.

Now there aren't five simple steps and it can't be achieved in a month. The perspective of the truth of this statement of Scripture is life long. Salvation is a journey, not a single point in time. Conversion and baptism open the door to the journey, but that is just the beginning. God never promised it would be simple or easy; the Apostle Peter could testify to that. But God has promised that in Christ we have all the resources we need to succeed. Don't be

120

misled by any false claims that offer you something quickly and with relative ease.

Mushrooms mature overnight; people take a lifetime, so don't be discouraged. You are of more value than many mushrooms. What you seek to achieve in your life spiritually is within your grasp, and probably more than you ever dreamed possible. Peter tells us that God has given us "exceeding great and precious promises, that through these you may be partakers of the divine nature, having escaped the corruption that is in the world through lust." What an amazing statement! God promises to give you two things- first, a means to escape the sinful corruptions that eat away at your soul, and second, the opportunity to participate in the divine nature. These two things God promises to you now.

You can have victory over your struggles, over the temptations and allure of what this world offers you in contrast to God. Now it doesn't say you won't have any more struggles or temptations, but that you will have escape from them. That is an important key to our living, knowing that failure isn't an ordained outcome. We don't have to be crushed under the weight of the temptations and pressures we face, which can so often be overwhelming. Peter writes to encourage believers living under threat and pressure, so his words are so relevant for us today. God can correct your vision. You can begin to see and understand that your soul can be satisfied in God alone. Other things that tempt you have no comparable value. The closer you draw to God, the weaker the grasp of temptation in your life.

But it doesn't stop there. Peter goes on to say that we may "become participants of the divine nature." What an amazing concept this is! No, it doesn't say, as some false cults teach today, that we actually become God, that we are absorbed into deity. You will never become God, but you can become all that God desires you to be as part of his divine re-creation. You become a God-like person, a Christ-like person in a miracle of grace and transformation. The Orthodox Church describes the mystery of such transformation in the term "theosis." This is our goal in Christ, what you are journeying toward, not a heavenly goal but one that can be attained here and now in the course of your life. In Christ this is within your grasp. Don't give up! Don't lose heart! God's divine power has given you what you need to achieve the goal.

Think, Respond And Apply
    You have completed this personal journey, this one month spiritual makeover. As you conclude this brief journey take some time to go back to day one and revisit questions 3 and 4.
    1. You were asked on day one, #3- "Write down what kind of a relationship you would really like to have with God and how you would like to have it impact your life." Read what you wrote in response on day one. Now reflect over the past month to consider what you have learned and achieved. Has there been any change in your desires or expectations? How are you progressing toward that kind of relationship you want to have with God?
    2. In #4 (of day one) you were asked to set some personal goals that would be realistic and achievable in developing the kind of relationship you desire with God. Take time to revisit these goals. Do you still hold to them now? Is there anything you would like to add to them or change in them as you progress from today at the end of the month? If so make the changes and at one month intervals go back and review the goals and see how you are doing.
    3. If you had not done so before this month, you have begun to keep a journal of this journey. Determine to continue with your journal, recording your daily thoughts, blessings, struggles and achievements. Write honestly from your heart and from time to time reflect back over what you have written to see where you have come from and where you are going. Be consistent and faithful.

Pray

Take some time for praise and worship in prayer today for what God has come to mean to you and what is happening in your life. This is a beginning. Pray that God would give you a heart to continue. Bring your hopes and fears before God with the assurance that God won't give up on you. They journey has just begun and you won't be on it alone.

FOOTNOTES

1. Saint Augustine, Confessions, trans. R.S. Pine Coffin, (Penguin Books, London, 1961) p.207

2. Saint Symeon the New Theologian, Hymn 13, trans. George A. Malney (DimensionBooks, Denville, n.d.), p.46

3. St John Cassian, "On The Holy Fathers of Sketis"' The Philokalia, vol.1 (Faber and Faber, London, 1979), p. 97

4. Saint Augustine, Confessions, trans. R. S. Pine Coffin, (Penguin Books, London 1961), pp. 21, 24

5. Fr. Theoklitos of Dionysiou, Between Heaven And Earth, (Astir, Athens, 1956), p. 83 6. Saint Symeon the New Theologian, Hymns of Divine Love I, trans. George A. Maloney (n.p., Denville, N.J. 1998), 156:168

7. Niketas Stethatos, Gnostic Chapters 46, Philokalia, vol.3 (Faber and Faber, London, 1979), p.337

8. Kallistos Ware, The Orthodox Way, (St. Vladimir's Seminary Press, N.Y., 1999), p.51

9. Makarios the Great, Fifty Spiritual Homilies,43.7, ed. Hermann Dorries, (DeGruyter, Berlin, 1964), p.289

10. Augustine, "Christian Compassion", The Sunday Sermons of the Great Fathers", vol. 2, (Henry Regnery Co., Chicago, 1958), p. 278

11. Diadochos of Photike, On Spiritual Knowledge, 59, Philokalia. vol.1, (Faber and Faber, London, 1979), p.251

12. Kallistos Ware, op. cit., p. 7

13. Aleksei Khomiakov, "The Church Is One", quoted in The Orthodox Way, Bishop Kallistos Ware (St. Vladimir Seminary Press, Crestwood, N.Y., 1995), p. 107

14. Cyprian of Carthage, "On The Unity Of The Church", Ante-Nicene Fathers, vol.5, (Hendrickson Publishers, Peabody, MA, 1999), p.422

15. I. M. Knotzevich, The Acquisition of the Holy Spirit, (St Herman of Alaska Brotherhood, Patina, CA, 1988), p. 82

16. Bishop Kallistos Ware, The Orthodox Way, (St Vladimir's Seminary Press, Crestwood, N.Y., 1995), p. 16

17. I. M. Kontzevitch, op. cit., pp. 35,36

18. Evagrios the Solitary, "On Prayer", The Philokalia, vol. 1, p. 60

19. St Mark The Ascetic, "On Spiritual Law", The Philokalia, vol. 1, p. 110, 116

20. Stefano Parenti, compiler, Praying With The Orthodox Tradition, (St. Vladimir's Seminary Press, Crestwood, N.Y., 1996), p.30

21. Kallistos Ware, op. cit., p. 116

22. John Chrysostom, Homily 13 in Matthew, uoted in The Sunday Sermons Of The Great Fathers, vol. 2, ed. M.F. Toal (Henry Regnery Co., Chicago, 1958), p.4

23. Stelios Ramfos, Like A Pelican In The Wilderness, (Holy Cross Orthodox Press, Brookline, MA, 2000), pp. 228, 230, 231

24. Kallistos Ware, op. cit., pp. 113-114

25. Stelios Ramfos, op. cit., p.7

26. Elder Ephriam, Counsels From The Holy Mountain, (St Anthony's Greek Orthodox Monastery, Florence, AZ, 1999), pp. 244,245

27. ibid., pp. 250, 251

28. Kallistos Ware, The Orthodox Church, (Penguin Books, N.Y., 1997), p. 265

29. St. John Chrysostom, "On Prayer", Sunday Sermons of the Great Fathers, vol. 2, pp. 396, 397

30. Jordan Bajis, Common Ground, (Light and Life Publishing, Minneapolis, 1996), p. 135

31. Mother Maria of Paris, quoted in "One, Of Great Price: The Life of Mother Maria of Ravensbruck", Sergi Hackel, (Darton, Longman and Todd, London, 1965), pp. 13, 29

32. Jordan Bajis, op. cit., pp. 125, 126

33. Niketas Stethatos, op. cit., p. 334

34. Makarios The Great, op. cit., p.50

For more
Regina Orthodox Press
Books, CDs and DVDs
Check our online catalogue

reginaorthodoxpress.com

Or call...

800 636 2470

Or write...

Regina Orthodox Press
PO BOX 5288
Salisbury MA 01952